Options Trading Crash Course 2022:

A Complete Beginner's Guide To Learn The Basics About Trading Options And Start Making Money In Just 30 Days

Ralph Riley

All trademarks inside this book are for clarifying purposes only and are possessed by the owners themselves, not allied with this document.

Disclaimer

All erudition supplied in this book are specified for educational and academic purpose only. The author is not in any way in charge of any outcomes that emerge from utilizing this book. Constructive efforts have been made to render information that is both precise and effective; however, the author is not to be held answerable for the accuracy or use/misuse of this information.

Foreword

I will like to thank you for taking the very first step of trusting me and deciding to purchase/read this life-transforming book. Thanks for investing your time and resources on this product.

I can assure you of precise outcomes if you will diligently follow the specific blueprint I lay bare in the information handbook you are currently checking out. It has transformed lives, and I firmly believe it will equally change your own life too.

All the information I provided in this Do It Yourself piece is easy to absorb and practice.

INTRODUCTION

Searching for a tremendous beginner-level book on options trading can be extremely frustrating because we have many people with different perspectives.

On the other side, consider that options trading as a fertile specific niche for originalities. This book, nevertheless, was written to take full advantage of clearness and readability, all while providing a comprehensive look at the principles of options trading. You should be ready to make your first few trades after reading this book.

In addition to helping develop a financier's portfolio, options trading involves a series of strategies that will permit financiers to incur considerable revenues at their designated convenience level.

How does one become an active options trader? Well, this is an excellent book to begin. Beginning with the basics, this guide to options trading will take budding investors through the definition of options, Infos on the various types of options, go through different strategies that can be implemented while trading, and set out an essential step-by-step guide to success, pointing out mistakes to prevent, and figuring out the investment terminology that frightens numerous prospective investors. Traders will be able to start with this book and jumpstart their professions in options trading and take theirs.

CHAPTER ONE

Understanding Stock Options

Trading on the stock exchange can be a complex organization with as much potential for loss as gain. Options are no exception and hence are most practical in the hands of a practiced and achieved trader.

Nevertheless, the financier who learns to use stock options to his or her benefit will be in a well-placed position when they sustain what is called risk capital. Which is the security that is a danger but may likewise yield vast amounts of revenue? This can be achieved by utilizing stock options to acquire an underlying asset.

So what precisely are stock options? The financial investment education website Investopedia defines it best as, "An option is a contract that gives the purchaser the right, but not the commitment, to buy or sell a hidden asset at a specific price on or before a certain date. Options similar to a stock or bond is security. Despite its many terms, options trading is much simpler than its definition. In other words, options trading is not just what the name recommends: it provides the trader options so that he or she can potentially sustain a minimal loss if an investment does not prove rewarding.

Here is an excellent example of options trading: Assume a trader chooses to acquire the stock for a new phone application that will allow users to purchase groceries while in transit. The trader may speculate that the worth of the security will increase due to the current shutdown of comparable applications and their business. The buyer and seller approach one another, who informs the financier that the security costs $2000.

However, the financier isn't sure of his forecast, and so he decides to buy the possession as an option for the cost of $400. From here, there are two possible outcomes. Firstly, the security may indeed increase as predicted and wished for that the trader being put in a commanding position because the individual who offered it to him is under the commitment to sell it to the buyer for $2000. Despite the truth that the security is now valued at a much higher rate; because the purchaser currently purchased the $400 option.

Nevertheless, the trader may have speculated improperly, which would cause the second potential results. If the rate of the security decreases, then the trader is under no commitment to buy the security but will lose the preliminary $400 premium. While that does not sound much of a loss like in this particular example, the numbers can change dramatically, relying on the property. The potential loss might be higher either since the options to purchase the property is very expensive (more top threat and cost regularly accompany the most appealing potential profit) or because the worth of the asset has dropped at a disconcerting rate. Also, things get more complicated when taking into account that the security might potentially rally. If the price does decline, it depends on the trader whether or not to go through with the agreement, which would usually be inadvisable, with the hope that the asset will reverse. The buyer can then offer it and earn a profit, or to enable the agreement to end and call the option premium loss at the end.

As implied, for instance, options are derivatives. They are called such because they originate from an underlying asset, which in this case, is the phone application stock. In reality, there is a range of underlying financial investments from which to select, such as stocks, equity, government securities, or indices.

It is essential to bear in mind though that options trading can also be used to offer securities. Also, in the manner of the same as the example above, if the trader thinks the price of security already in their ownership is going to decrease, they can sell it for what is hopefully an attractive option if they are not able to offer it outright.

However, as indicated by the meaning, there are options trading requirements that might either hinder the trader or be helpful. The buyer is never bound to buy the security if the worth of the security is not increasing as hoped.

If the security is increasing, the buyer always has the right to buy the guard at the cost guaranteed by the seller. This is something that ought to be taken into the mind to consider whenever selling options, as it can result in a high loss, considering that the seller is continuously bound to sell the options to the purchaser within the parameters of the agreement Options trading includes due dates. The purchaser can buy the security before or on the date of expiration, which is agreed upon by the purchaser and seller when the contract is developed. If the expiration date passes, the purchaser will lose the initial investment. When it comes to a specific selling the option, they would get just the initial investment from the buyer and then be free to offer the security at another price ultimately.

Essentially, trading options is just an agreement. The function of the contract is to purchase or offer an underlying asset, which, in the example, is the phone application security. If the expiration date for the options passes, the seller is free to produce a brand-new one with a brand-new buyer.

Thus, options trading provides a way for purchasers to hedge their bets on the planet of investments. While the risks might race high, an accomplished trader might have the ability to use options trading to decrease potential losses, as opposed to trading just using methods that have countless dangers. Just like many other aspects of life, education is essential to end up being a wise and rewarding financier.

Protecting financial investment profits is accomplished by hedging investments, a fantastic ability that will permit the knowledgeable trader to reduce losses while enjoying the full advantages of gratitude. The downfall in hedging is that it costs money; there is no method to protect properties versus losses without paying some type of premium. This ends up being complicated extremely quickly because hedging an investment requires making an extra, adversely associating investment. Despite this, hedging remains a prevalent strategy amongst financiers, which is since options are a notoriously severe danger. Hedging does not assist in increasing possible earnings, only to reduce risk; therefore, it is best used with the high risk/high return securities previously pointed out.

Having the ability to manage underlying possessions utilizing options is likewise described as leveraging. Also, to hedging, it is one of the primary draws to options trading, as leveraging allows the trader to manage a large amount of cash with extremely little financial investment. Further speculation of that financial investment can then lead the trader to either let the options agreement end and therefore only lose the initial option premium or force the seller to cost the full strike cost As discussed before though, leveraging can work as a double-edged sword if preventative measures are not taken, whether they are hedging, picking suitable strategies to increase the investment, or having a precise exit technique.

When trading, options may be positioned into particular classifications. This is because options are defined by five key components, a few of which have already been mentioned; they are the underlying security, kind of possibilities, strike rate, expiration date, and system of trade. The components that are yet detailed are easily specified. There are two kinds of options called puts and calls, which will be discussed in the next chapter. The strike cost is merely the price agreed upon by the purchaser and seller at which to sell the hidden security. In the example, the strike rate was $2000. The unit of trade represents several shares, which is a portion of ownership by an individual in a corporation or other monetary investment that entitles the investor to a relative quantity of the profits. One must bear in mind that a person option agreement represents 100 shares.

CHAPTER TWO

In this chapter, we will check out the numerous kinds of options that are offered and how they work. By the end of the episode, we will present some various types of options that are available, consisting of business provided options and index options and how they vary from exchange-traded stock options summary of call options and put options.

The two primary types of options are call options and put options. A call option is the right to buy 100 shares of the underlying stock, and a put option is the right to sell 100 shares of an underlying stock.

Market value intrinsic value of options decreases as the marketplace worth of stock of the underlying stock decreases. If the marketplace worth of the underlying stock is below the strike cost, exercising your option would result in purchasing the underlying stock at a price more significant than the present market worth. Therefore, the opportunity has no intrinsic value, and modifications in the options price will represent a fall in time worth just.

Revenue is figured out by the increase in the market value of the underlying stock, less the premium paid, and loss of time value.

Income is restricted to the premium got. Losses are possibly unlimited; however, just happen if the option is cost a loss or worked out against the seller. They were speculating that the market worth of the underlying stock will increase.

It was knowing that the market worth of the underlying stock will stay stable or fall.

Option buyers (takers).

An investor or trader who wishes to buy options is generally anticipating a considerable movement in the rate of the underlying security before the expiry date of the options. Options supply the buyer with the chance to benefit from this expected rate motion, without needing to offer capital to cover the complete expense of the hidden security. However, this takes advantage of does come with a cost inherent in the time worth of the options.

Options likewise supply option purchasers with minimal risk. Their maximum loss on any options trade will be the amount they pay for the option (plus deal costs). For instance, let's assume you acquire a call option on CBA for $1, and over the next couple of weeks, the price of CBA falls by $2. If you had acquired the CBA shares, you would have lost $2 per share. Nevertheless, by purchasing the options, your loss is always limited to the options premium you paid, which, in this case, is $1 per share.

Tip.

The buyer of options pays a premium to obtain the right to purchase or offer the underlying securities. This premium represents both the expense of the optimum and the right possible loss on this deal. No matter the motion in the market value of the underlying security, the options purchaser's maximum failure on taking an option is the premium they spent for the options.

It is imperative to bear in mind that option purchasers have the right; however, not the obligation to exercise their options. If the option holder does not want to work out the options and effect a transfer to the underlying stock, they can liquidate their position (effectively sell their options).

According to the ASX, as of November 2010, usually, just 15 percent of all options traded on the exchange are worked out. Of the staying 85 percent, 60 percent of.

These are closed out, and 25 percent end useless. A significant number of options were bought and offered by financiers and traders for functions other than getting the underlying stock.

Options sellers.

Option authors charge a premium for offering options. Numerous options authors provide options to produce earnings from the option premiums. As an outcome, these options authors usually are anticipating that the price of the underlying security will remain flat or stable. This will result in the option of losing worth as the time worth of the option decreases.

Option authors may also be aiming to create a more significant benefit from the movement in the underlying security. The author of call options will be speculating on a fall in the cost of the hidden safe, and the author of put options will be thinking on the increase in the value of the underlying security.

As the options to work out rests with the buyer, option authors can have their options worked out at any time before expiration. They will not know if or when their choices may be exercised. They are more most likely to be applied when the options are 'in-the-money' and close to expiry. An OPTION is in-the-money when it includes intrinsic value. That is, for a call options, the marketplace worth is above the strike cost of the option, and for a put options, the marketplace worth is listed below the strike price of the opportunity.

Option authors also bring a much higher level of risk compared to options purchasers. Whereas the maximum chance for the buyer of the option is restricted to the option premium, the situation is quite different for options authors. An author of exposed call options is, in theory, exposed to unrestricted threat as they are exposed to boosts in the worth of the underlying stock. As the marketplace worth of the underlying stock boosts, the option author has the threat of needing to buy the underlying stock at its market worth, nevertheless high that might be.

A put options author is exposed to the worth of the underlying stock at the strike rate. If it is worked out at the strike price, the author of the option has the responsibility to purchase this stock from the option holder. If the market worth of the stock falls to absolutely no and the option is worked out, the holder of the options is required to buy the useless stock from the option holder at the strike rate.

Call options.

A call option is the right to buy 100 shares of the underlying stock at the strike cost. When they acquire the option until the expiration date of options, this right can be exercised by the taker (purchaser) of options at any time.

Buyer of call options.

By purchasing a call option, you will produce a profit on your options if the market worth of the underlying stock increases by sufficient to cover the premium you spent for the call option and any decrease in time worth that happens while you hold the option. This boost in market value must happen before the expiry date of your options, the purchaser of a call option deals with a time deadline in which to produce a benefit from the transaction. If you chose to purchase the underlying stock straight, you could wait for your forecasted increase in market price to understand a revenue on your financial investment. However, by buying call options over the same stock, you do not have this advantage. You will stop working to generate earnings on your call options if the market value of the underlying stock does not increase by an adequate quantity before the expiry date of the call options.

Tip.

Time is a crucial aspect in identifying if an option purchaser generates make money from their call option. The market worth of the underlying stock must increase by an adequate.

Quantity before the expiry date for the buyer of a call Options, to realize revenue on their financial investment.

The purchaser of a call option is speculating (and hoping!) that the marketplace value of the underlying stock will increase in worth before the expiration date of the option. If the worth of the market underlying stock increases and the strike cost is less than the market value of the underlying stock, the quality of the option will also increase. This implies that the purchaser of the call option can either offer the call at a profit, or get the stock below the price of the present market worth.

Sellers of options call.

The call option sellers are maybe hoping that the market value of the underlying stock will fall or remain flat, as this will result in a decrease in the worth of the call option. The seller can then redeem the options at a lower cost and understand a profit. If the underlying stock is valued and listed below the strike rate of the options, it is extremely not likely that the options will be worked out. The purchaser of the call options is not going to buy the stock at a price higher than the current market price! On this occasion, the seller will merely wait up until the expiry date, at which time the options will end worthless. For this instance, the seller could retain the premium they got on the initial sale of the option as a revenue.

Comprehending call options from a seller's point of view is a bit harder to begin with. As a purchaser of a call option, you are following a buy-hold-sell pattern, which is much the same as buying the stock directly. The main distinctions are the ability to expose yourself to the stock at a fraction of the cost of the capital, and you have a restricted time duration to sell or exercise your option.

When offering a call option, you are reversing this pattern and following a sequence of sell-hold-buy, or simply sell-hold. You are providing your options first, expecting the price of your option to fall and then repurchasing it at a lower rate.

Or even much better still, you sell-hold, and if the option has no intrinsic worth at expiry, you have no need to redeem at all.

Put options

A put option offers the option buyer the right to sell 100 shares of the underlying stock at the strike cost. When they buy the options until the expiration date of options, this right can be exercised by the taker (purchaser) of the options at any time.

Buyers of put options

The worth of a put option will increase as the market value of the hidden security reduces listed below the strike cost of the option. The option holder has the right to offer their stock at a set rate, even though the market worth of the stock is falling. If the underlying stock market value of the falls by enough to cover the premium you paid for the, by buying put options, you will create revenue on your option put option. This fall in market value with all option, needs to happen before the expiration date of your option.

Put options supply the option purchaser with an opportunity to speculate on falls in the market's worth of stock. Thinking on falls in-stock rates straight in the stock exchange is described as trading short or short selling. Short selling of shares straight can be pricey and tough. Put options can effectively provide the means for buying quick. As soon as again, time is an aspect to think about when trading or investing in options. To produce earnings on your put option, the marketplace worth of the underlying stock should decrease by a sufficient amount before the expiry date of the put option.

Tip

Put options can be useful to protect earnings on your existing stock holdings. The premium can be thought about to be like paying for insurance against losses a fall in the marketplace value of your shares.

The put option buyer is speculating that the marketplace worth of the underlying stock will reduce in quality before the expiration date of the options. If the underlying stock market value decreases, the variety of the option will increase (if the options are in-the-money). This means that the put option buyer can either sell the put options at earnings or, if they hold the underlying security, sell this stock at a price above the present market worth.

Instead of speculating, the buyer of a put option may purely also be taking the option position to secure profits on existing shareholdings. If shares they hold have experienced a current increase in price and they think that the stock worth will fall in the brief term, rather than offering their stock, they could buy a put option that would secure their revenue. The fall in the value of their stock holding would be balanced out in part by the gain on their put options if the market worth of the underlying stock did fall.

Put options sellers

The put option seller hopes that the market value of the underlying stock will increase or stay flat, as this will lead to a decrease in the value of the put options. The seller can then redeem the options at a lower cost and understand a revenue. Additionally, if the value of the underlying stock is above the strike rate of the option, it is highly not likely that the option will be exercised. The purchaser of the put option is not going to offer their stock at a price lower than the present market cost! On this occasion, the seller will just wait until the expiry date, at which time the option will expire uselessly. The seller would keep the premium they received on the preliminary sale of the option as a profit.

When offering put options, as merely selling call options, you are following a series of sell-hold-buy or just sell-hold. You are providing your options initially, hoping for the price of the option to fall and then repurchasing it at a lower rate. Or, still better, you sell-hold, and if the market worth of the hidden security is above the strike rate, the option has no intrinsic value, and you have no need to purchase back at all.

Company issued options

The business released options are options that are issued straight by a business. The company sets the conditions and terms of the options, and they are not noted on an exchange. Usually, these options are issued to existing shareholders or crucial workers for the functions of raising additional capital. These options offer the shareholders the right to buy new shares at a set cost (workout rate) before a set date. In these circumstances, the business is the author of the options. And an obligation to fulfill any options that are exercised.

As the private companies provide these options for particular purposes, the terms and conditions of these options are figured out by the company issuing the options. Therefore, the conditions and terms, including the expiration date, workout rate, and several shares covered per option, will vary. You require to read the paperwork thoroughly to determine the terms and conditions and the treatments needed to work out the option if you are released these types of options.

Index Options

Options over a share price is called Index options. An index price is shared in a group of noted shares. Each share in the index is provided a calculation, and weighting is done using their weighting and current market cost to identify the index value. This index value is revealed in points.

Index options offer you direct exposure to a group of securities that consist of the share market index. This enables you to trade a position on the market as a whole, or the marketplace sector or business that make up the index you wish to purchase.

The Australia options, which is ASX options over the S&P/ ASX 200 index. This is an index that is computed based upon the top 200 companies noted on the ASX—trading these options successfully exposes you to movements in the total Australian stock exchange.

The worth of your index options will differ with motions in the quality of the index, which is reflective of the total value of the group of securities it represents. Moves in the S&P/ ASX 200 index are viewed as reflective of the movement in the overall sharemarket, as this index covers the most prominent 200 stocks noted on the ASX.

There are a few distinctions to keep in mind between index options and stock options, which we will now go over.

Index options are European design options. This implies that index options can not be worked out before the settlement date. You can, nevertheless, purchase and sell them before the workout date. Being European design options likewise suggests that there is no threat of new exercise for the seller. The sellers of index options do not require to fret about their options being exercised before the expiration date.

Index options are cash-settled. This suggests that the value of the index options is determined on the settlement date, and upon exercise, all options are closed out with the pertinent cash value. You will be paid the worth if your index option agreement is worth something. If your index option has no quality on the expiry date, it merely ends uselessly. The money quantity you receive on expiry is the distinction between the settlement worth of the exercise and the index worth of the index. If your index options are in-the-money, you will only receive a cash worth settlement value on expiry that is computed utilizing opening rates.

The settlement amount is computed using the initial rate of each stock in the underlying index on the expiry date early morning. For every stock in the index, the first traded cost or opening price is taped for each stock in the index. The value of the index is then determined to use these initial values.

The premium and standard index options prices in points are expressed. The index itself is a pointedly expressed, so it follows that the premium and strike rate of index options is also revealed in positions. Each index has multiplier in an index, which converts these indicate a dollar worth estimated at a premium of 20 points would cost you $500 to buy (20 points × the index multiplier of $25 = $500). Likewise, the value of an index option agreement is calculated as the strike price of the option increased by the index multiplier.

Advantages of index options

There are a variety of crucial advantages in purchasing index options. The same benefits of investing in share options that we talked about in chapter 1 also apply to index options. They are risk management, speculation, income, diversity, and leverage generation.

There are likewise some extra advantages you can achieve from trading or capitalizing options in index.

Broader market exposure

We are representing an index of a large parcel of stocks. Therefore, the index is frequently representative of the market as a whole or an essential sector of the market. Investing in index options enables you to purchase an option that tracks a specific index successfully.

This will approximate an investment because of a specific parcel of stocks, providing you direct exposure to a broader market. In this instance, you have the advantage of diversification as your investment does not bring risk connected to a particular business. This may be offset by the primary market motion of all the other companies in the index if one company in the index does not carry out well. You may benefit from being exposed to the broad market represented by the index, without needing to purchase each of the individual stocks that make up that particular index.

Portfolio Defense

Investors who hold shares of a portfolio may wish to combat the effect of a market recession without having to offer their shares. Taxation on the realization of the financial investment gain, plus deal expenses, are two reasons why a financier may consider using options, and in specific index options, to protect their share portfolio.

If the market portfolio does not fall in worth declines as an outcome, buying index put options can provide the financier with some settlement. The increase in the worth of their put options will balance out the fall in the value of their portfolio.

As alluded to in the past, there are numerous kinds of options from which a trader can take advantage that will then allow him or her to sell or purchase options. Also, there are subcategories of options with various stipulations and benefits. It is crucial to examine and be familiar with these to use options for optimum profit.

Traders keep in mind would do well to that options trading does take a lot of practice and just those who are well versed in options trading and mindful of the motion and trends of business and monetary institutions succeed in this specific sect of trading. Being said that, here are the various categories and subcategories of options trading. Every two items listed are combined with one another. The call option opposite is a put options, and the opposite of the American options is European options.

Calls: This is a type of options used in the example in the previous chapter. Calls are used by buyers, implying that if a trader has a call option, they have the right, however, are not bound to purchase an underlying property at the strike cost before a formerly agreed-upon the date expiration.

The trader always wants the buyer to value of the hidden asset to appreciate exponentially so that they can purchase the underlying possession at a strike cost that is much cheaper than the value of the security and, after that, offer the hidden ownership for enormous revenue. In-, at-, and out-of-the-money is another term for this. When the value of the hidden possession is higher than the strike price, the purchaser is in-the-money. When the worth is the same as the strike cost, the buyer is at-the-money, and they are out-of-the-money when the value is listed below the strike price.

Puts: Puts are the opposite of calls. Having put options implies the trader is a seller. In this case, the seller will expect the rate of the hidden possession dropping and will sell it at a high price before the cost drops, therefore gaining a profit. The price will require to drop before the expiration date and is the catch for the seller.

If this happens, then the buyer will likely have paid the seller the full strike rate, which will be more than the worth of the property.

The initial seller gain will be options premium used to secure the contract if the cost drops after the expiration date, nevertheless. This likewise means the seller is probably losing money on the underlying property, which they still own. There are two more catches to offering puts, and they both come down to the purchasers right, however not the responsibility, to bring out the options contract. If the rate plummets excessive before the option contract's expiration date, the purchaser may choose to give up purchasing the hidden security, and the seller will be entrusted just the premium as a reward. However, if the seller composes a put as part of a strategy, they will need to remember that the put can invariably be designated, and the investor will be required to offer. In concerns to the-- in, -at, and-- out-of-the-cash terms, the precise opposite of calls is exact of puts.

Before proceeding to the other kinds of options, here is a quick note concerning some short information relating to those who take part in options trading. There are four positions that can be held that fall into two categories. The very first category is made up of the "holders" and consists of those who buy calls and puts. The 2nd consists of "writers" who offer calls and puts. This is similar to what is referred to as long and short positions within the stock exchange, respectively. As specified in the past, the most crucial differentiation between the holders and writers (buyers and sellers) is those holders always buy but are never obliged to do so. In contrast, the obligated writers to buy or sell, which tends to make the writing position a hazardous one. This is less confusing as is it becomes these principles are talked about even more in later chapters of this book.

American Options: The very first thing to keep in mind when thinking about European and American options is that the kind of options bears no relation to geographical areas. The titles differentiate merely are the two types of options. Having specified this, American options are the most typically traded one, since they can be redeemed at any time during the life of the option, even up to maturity, likewise called the expiration date. This flexibility allows buyers to acquire the options when the worth is above the strike cost well before the expiration date, removing the chances that the worth will drop and the buyer will lose on the original amount they paid to buy the option. American options typically reach their expiration date on the 3rd Friday of the month.

European Options: options European differentiate from their American equivalents because the buyer or seller may exercise their rights only at the option's maturity. This enables far less flexibility and requires the trader to be incredibly positive of their position before participating in the acquired options contract. A crucial point of European options is that unlike American options, the expiration date is always on the last Thursday of the month.

Index Options: Index options follow the very same general principle meaning as stock options, with one significant difference: traded on indices options are. Popular options index to trade on are the S&P 500 Index, the Russell 2000 Index, the NASDAQ-100 Index, and on perhaps the most well-known index, the Dow Jones Industrial Average. The premium is usually settled in money. Also, index options are not consistently available. For instance, European-style index options are typically traded, however only minimal indices, such as the S&P 500, will use American-style options.

Equity Options: Equity in itself, usually speaking, is the value of the property minus the worth of that property's liabilities. In this case, aptly defines Investopedia equity options, also understood as equity derivative, as "an acquired instrument with underlying possessions based upon equity securities. An equity derivative's worth will fluctuate with changes in its underlying possession's equity, which is usually measured by share cost" (Investopedia, Equity Derivative). This can also be believed of as purchasing or offering options for a corporation's stock.

Short-Term Options: This is the kind of option that was used in the example. With short options, the expiration date for the option can be anywhere from a couple of minutes to a few days into the future. This all depends upon the agreement concurred upon in between the buyer and seller. Success in short-term options trading is dependent upon the instinct of the trader and his/her knowledge of the marketplace and underlying properties. For example, a trader who is well notified relating to only technology would not wish to buy a short-term option for a share of a growing art repair company. Instead, the trader should either adhere to what she or he knows or end up being informed about locations which the investor is interested in pursuing. Education is recommended, given that it expands the scope for success.

LEAP: For the functions of education, it may be practical for starting stock option traders to believe in LEAPs as long-lasting options. LEAP, which is mainly for Long-term Equity Anticipation Securities, stands advantageous for long-term investors because the expiration date maybe 39 months. With an extreme such length of time, there is an opportunity for higher fluidity and flexibility, permitting the worth of the asset to grow or perhaps recuperate if it diminishes throughout the life of the agreement.

Everyday Vanilla Options: This name is a fundamental description for an option with no included benefits or terms. When the options are offered, the kind of options (call or put), expiration date, strike price, and single hidden asset are currently figured out. Furthermore, "the options are effective at the existing date, and when exercised, its payoff equates to the difference in between the worth of the underlying possession and the strike cost" (Financial Dictionary). This is an appealing option due to its pure nature and is generally found as an exchange-traded option. As the most common and necessary options available, it is a popular and sensible starting place for newbie options traders.

Unique Options: A popular over-the-counter option, exotic options offer buyers and sellers the chance to include and customize acquired contracts on any extra stipulations at their discretion. With so many more balls to juggle, traders must be familiar with the market before venturing into exotic options. Different from European and American options, this kind of agreement can vary in terms of the hidden asset, expiration date, and strike cost.

For instance, if a buyer telephones for an option in which he pays the seller $400 for the option and agrees with the seller that the strike price is $2000 at an expiration date of 3 days from when the option was purchased, they can include another stipulation to it. In this case, state that the terms are that the agreement does not enter into effect until the value of the stock reaches a certain rate point. The buyer would not deserve to acquire the options until the worth of the stock reached the formerly concurred upon the mark. This is just one of the numerous variations of exotic options, all of which require to be studied meticulously before being put into usage.

Exchange-Traded Options: The options are majorly traded through an exchange, such as the Chicago Stock Exchange, therefore exchange-traded options, also called noted stock options, fall under this classification. The merits of an exchange-traded option is that the hidden possession, strike rate, expiration date, and quantity can be viewed in advance because they belong to a standardized agreement. This is also a feasible options because taking part in a contract using an established exchange guarantees that the individuals can use the clearinghouse. As a clearinghouse member, the trader is accountable for reporting positions at the end of the day and also keeping an adequate quantity of money. That shows the trader's place in a debit account. While this may sound extraneous and confusing, the settle is that the clearinghouse is responsible for agreements being satisfied, and thus the trader getting paid. Essentially, a clearinghouse is an intermediary between sellers and purchasers.

Over-the-Counter Options: These are options contracts that are created beyond an established trading group, thus the name. Also called OTC options,

non-prescription option "has a direct link in between the purchaser and seller, has no secondary market, and has no standardization of striking prices and expiration dates" (Nasdaq, Over-the-Counter Option). The downside here is that the buyer or seller would require to actively look for potential organization partners with whom to make a transaction instead of just choosing options to buy from a currently available list. The benefit of OTC options lies in the ability to tailor the crucial components. Therefore a buyer and seller might work out long positions for later expiration dates or perhaps swap the strike cost. Nevertheless, the contract requires to be taped in a dependable method since OTC options do not use the thanks to a clearinghouse to assist settle debts; the purchaser and seller must exchange funds themselves.

CHAPTER THREE

In this chapter, we will outline a few of the primary benefits of trading in options and why you may consider purchasing or offering options as a part of your total trading method. We will also discuss the significant dangers in buying and providing options, remembering that the threats included in options are substantially various for buyers of options compared with the risks for sellers of options.

Benefits of option trading

When purchasing options, you are investing in an asset with no real worth, with a minimal life, and which may be worthless within a few months. As you will quickly find, there are numerous benefits of trading options that can be used in a wide variety of methods.

We will now describe a few of the main advantages of options. These are extended attributes that apply to options. As we talk about the types of options in more detail and the methods that can be used for each kind of options, you will see the benefits (and drawbacks) of trading options.

It is likewise fascinating to keep in mind that a benefit to a seller will typically equate as a downside to the buyer and vice versa. The factor this operates in the marketplace is, the reason or strategy used by the seller is different from the idea the purchaser has participated in the agreement.

Tips

When evaluating the benefits of using options, you likewise need to think about the risks associated with your particular options method.

The benefits we will talk about are:

- Danger management
- Speculation
- Leverage
- Diversification
- Income Generation.

Danger Management

Options provide financiers with the ability to manage danger within their portfolio. Options can provide a financier with a hedge versus falls in the price of their present stock holdings. It can effectively allow a financier to lock in some profits on their holding, without needing to sell their shares physically.

This can be useful when an investor wishes to maintain their shares for a longer-term or does not want to understand a capital gain by offering their investment at the current time.

Purchasing a put option allows you to buy the right to sell your present shares at an advantageous price if you are anticipating a fall in the cost of those shares before the expiry date of the option. The investors are allowed to make a gain on the put options that will offset a loss on the physical shares, on the occasion that the stocks do fall in value.

You own 3000 shares in a stock presently trading at $10.50. You want to secure some revenue at this price as you feel that the price is most likely to fall in the brief term. To use this strategy, you purchase 30 put option agreements with a strike cost of $10.50. This costs you to buy $0.20 per share contained in each agreement (with 100 shares in each transaction).

This purchase provides you the right to offer 3000 shares at $10.50 whenever before the options expiry date. Your put option value will increase by a similar quantity (less any ended time worth) if the stock rate subsequently falls. Thus you are safeguarding yourself against a fall in the price of your stock. A fall in worth of your stock will be balanced by a rise in the value of your options.

If the stock cost stays at or above $10.50, then you would either not exercise your options or sell your option close to the expiration date (although it would deserve very little).

If the stock rate does fall to, state, $9.50, then the worth of your put options would increase by $1.00 (less any expired time worth). You could then offer these options for approximately $1.00 and realize earnings of $3000.00. This will balance out the fall in worth of your shareholding of a similar amount. Effectively, you have paid $600.00 for your options to Defend you against the fall in the price of stock position.

Speculation

The capability to trade online and the listing of options on the ASX make it very simple to purchase and offer options. The options trading makes it possible for traders at ease to buy an option contract with the intent of selling the options before the expiration date for a revenue. The traders may have expectations of an increase in the rate of the option (due to a change in the cost of the underlying security). And no objective of ever exercising the option if your option has intrinsic value, the value of your options will change much in line with the change in worth of the underlying stock. You will also see a fall in quality that is unrelated to any change in worth of the hidden security but is due to a fall in the time value of the option as it nears expiry.

How option move with changes in the value of the underlying stock?. These movements are for options that have an intrinsic worth in their premium.

As a speculator, you can acquire call options if you are expecting the rate of the underlying security to increase. As the underlying price of security rises, the intrinsic value of your options will increase by a similar amount if you are anticipating the rate of the underlying security to fall, your method may be to buy put options as the price of the underlying security drops. The intrinsic options value will increase by a similar amount. To produce a profit, you need the worth of the underlying security to move in your favor before the expiry date, and you would need to offer your option on or before the expiration date.

When purchasing and after offering American style stock options as a method to generate short-term revenue, you need to ensure you sell your options before the expiry date. This requires the cost of the underlying stock to move in your favor before the expiry date.

Leverage

Leverage is the ability to produce the same level of return from a prospective financial investment; however, utilizing a smaller sized initial expense. If you owned the real shares, Purchasing a call option with intrinsic value exposes you to a comparable gain or loss that you would attain. The cost of a fraction of the price options of the underlying stock. This permits you to benefit from changes in the value of the stock without paying the full fee of the capital.

Leverage does come with a new threat; the gains are amplified through the usage, so too are any losses. Some examples show how force can create a more significant portion return than can direct financial investment.

Your returned percentage can be magnified as a result of the leverage achieved through the usage of options. It is necessary to note that your losses can be equally magnified in some circumstances. Nevertheless, when purchasing options, your loss will always be limited to the premium you spent on the opportunity.

Idea

When speculating using options, you need to represent the fall in time worth of your option and your deal costs when assessing your trading opportunity.

Diversification

The use of options can offer you the opportunity to benefit from the motion in the rate of a stock at a portion of the stock price. This permits you to construct a varied portfolio for a lower preliminary expense. This comes at a cost as your options include a value for the time of expiry, which will decrease to no over the life of the option.

Income generation

When selling an option, you get an advance premium from the purchaser of your option. The premium kept, whether or not the option has worked out. This premium can produce an income stream if carefully selected options are sold on a systematic basis. The seller maintains the premium and has no further commitment if the options are not exercised.

There are several methods based on offering options to generate premium income. The goal is to sell options that are not likely to be worked out, or purchase back (closeout) your options before the expiration date if there is a danger they will be exercised.

CHAPTER FOUR

Risks of Option Trading

Although there are various advantages to options, like all monetary investments, there are also risks related to trading in options. The threats differ, relying on the type of option and are somewhat different for the seller and the purchaser.

Similar to any financial investment, you should just trade options if you comprehend how they work and how they fit with your overall trading or investment technique. Besides, there are a variety of threats that specify options that you must know and prepared to manage.

The dangers we will talk about are:

- Market danger
- Risk of expiring useless
- Threat due to leverage
- Potential for limitless losses (as a seller of options).
- Danger of margin calls (as a seller of options).
- Liquidity danger.

Market danger.

For the buyer of an options, market risk is the threat that the marketplace value of your options will decrease, therefore stagnating in line with your expectation or speculation. The market value of your options is mainly impacted by the market price of the underlying security but is likewise affected by the time of expiration—the volatility of the cost of the hidden security and even motions in the rate of interest.

The market threat for the option author is the risk that the marketplace value of the underlying shares will transfer to develop or increase the intrinsic worth of the option. This will increase the opportunity of the option being worked out or create a loss for the seller in closing their position.

You require to ensure you have a plan to manage your market threat and have a method if the value of your options does stagnate in your direction. Option pricing is gone over in more information in the danger of expiring worthless.

The expiration date is the day on which you need to either sell the option, or exercise the to expire uselessly. If an option is without intrinsic value, the worth of the option will reduce as you approach the expiration date, and your time value deteriorates (this is referred to as time decay).

The intrinsic worth will just exist in an option in the following circumstances:

For call options, the intrinsic worth will be inherent when the strike price of the option is lower than the market worth of the underlying stock. The value intrinsic will then equal to the difference in these two amounts. This develops because you have the option to purchase the underlying stock at a rate listed below the current market price.

For put options, the scenario is the reverse. Your option will have value intrinsic when the market worth of the underlying stock is listed below the strike price of the option.

The risk of an expiring option worthless is a threat that the buyer of an option needs to bear. This is an advantage for the seller, as they profit from the option premium they gather when an option expires useless.

Risk due to use.

Simply as leverage has the prospective to amplify your earnings on a trade, use equally can magnify your losses. A reasonably small change in the value of the underlying security can lead to a significant portion change in the value of the option. When purchasing an option, the option rate is only a portion of the price of the underlying stock; nevertheless, your revenue or loss on the option is close to the quantity you would make if you had traded the underlying stock at its full value.

Tip.

Although leverage can amplify your revenue or loss on an option contract, when purchasing options, your damage is always limited to the premium you spent for the option.

Possible for endless losses (as a seller of options).

Sellers of options take the responsibility to offer (call options) or buy (put options) the underlying stock at the strike cost if the option is worked out by the buyer of the options. If you have offered call options, you commit to providing the underlying stock at the strike cost if your choice is worked out by the buyer. You are losing the value between the present market cost of the strike and the stock price if you currently own the stock. You have offered an exposed option if you do not own the underlying stock. You will need to purchase the stock on the market at the current market value and deliver it to the option buyer who has worked out the option. As the marketplace value of the underlying stock has no theoretical limit, your losses on selling exposed call options are potentially endless.

As a put options seller, you have the responsibility to purchase the underlying stock at the strike rate if the purchaser exercises your option. If the marketplace worth of the underlying stock was up to or near absolutely no, you are still obliged to buy the stock, which is nearly useless at the strike cost. As the underlying stock cost can just fall to absolutely no, your losses as a seller of put options are only limited to the value of the underlying stock at the strike cost.

Risk of margin calls (as an option seller).

When you offer an option, you are required to provide security (referred to as a margin) to show that you can fulfill your responsibilities if the option is exercised. This margin can be in the type of the security underlying (if a call option), other collateral or cash value. If option increases in value, thus breaking you as a seller, you may be required to offer additional margin to cover the boost in your responsibility.

Typically, margins are needed to be paid within 24 hours, but your broker sets this time frame. If you fail to supply an additional margin upon demand within the required amount of time, your broker will have the ability to close out your option position or liquidate some or all of your existing shareholdings to satisfy your margin requirements.

Liquidity risk.

Market makers are the firms that offer quote prices (cost you get on selling an option) and deal costs (cost you pay on buying an option) for an option in a range. They will provide an options market for the most part; nevertheless, they do have the scope in terms of the rates, number of options, and times that they need to price estimate a bid and ask the cost for an option.

Tip.

In times of high volatility, the cost of your options might not move as you expect. The value of the underlying security might relocate your instructions; nevertheless, the option value may be adjusted for the threat of significant movement in the underlying security (the high volatility), suggesting that your option position does not reflect any earnings on the transaction.

CHAPTER FIVE

The marketplace forces affecting the worth of stocks will, later on, impact the marketplace worth of the options attached to those stocks. The option itself has no underlying quality-- its value is obtained from the worth of the capital and your capability to buy or offer that stock.

In this chapter, explore we shall on the two components of an option rate. These parts are intrinsic worth and time value. We will look at the areas that impact the price of options, and how these areas vary from the aspects which affect the cost of a stock.

Stock rates versus option prices

Stocks provided by a company are limited in number, and as a result, their price is influenced by the forces of demand and supply. Like any limited product, if more individuals desire to buy a stock than individuals willing to sell, the rate will naturally increase. Likewise, if more people want to offer their stocks, and there are few buyers, the stock price will fall. The most extreme example of this is during a stock exchange crash, or correction, where sellers are flooding the market and, in the lack of any substantial purchasers, the rate falls dramatically.

Broadly, influence in the stock price by the performance (both actual and expected) of the company and all the industrial and financial elements that affect that real and anticipated performance.

With exchange-traded options, the exchange will permit investors to sell any number and buy options. They are not constrained by the variety of shares released of the underlying stock. Therefore, the price of options is impacted only indirectly by the forces of supply and need as they are not a restricted product.

The option value is mainly affected by the movement in the rate of the stock underlying, and by the time of passage. These factors are known as intrinsic value and time worth. To add further intricacy on various factors will affect the intrinsic value and the time value of any option price.

Option premium = intrinsic value + time worth

Intrinsic worth

Intrinsic value is the difference between the marketplace worth of the underlying stock and the strike value of the option. This is the most quickly understood element of an option cost as it represents a specified advantage that can be easily measured.

Intrinsic worth represents the ability to offer an underlying share above the marketplace cost (put option) or to purchase the underlying stock below the current market value (call option).

In-the-money options

Options that have intrinsic value in their rates are referred to as being 'in-the-money.' For call options, this suggests that the strike price of the option is listed below the current market price of the hidden share; therefore, there is value in working out the option. The value intrinsic is present as the option holder can exercise their option and buy the hidden shares for a rate lower than they might on the marketplace.

Out-of-the-money options.

Options that have no intrinsic worth in their pricing are described as being 'out-of-the-money.' For call options, this implies that the strike rate is above the current market value; therefore, there is no value in working out the option. There is no merit to buy shares at a price more significant than you might pay on the free market.

Call options offer the purchaser the right; however, not the responsibility to buy the hidden shares. It is better to purchase the shares on the share market directly if your options are out-of-the-money, and you wish to acquire the secret shares.

Option rates Suggestion.

Put options offer the buyer with the right; however, not the obligation to sell the hidden shares. If your options are out-of-the-money and wish you to sell your shares, it is much better to sell them on the sharemarket straight.

As suggests the name, an at-the-money option is an option where the strike rate of the option is equal to the current market price of the underlying shares. Let's consider this, as an example:

You are considering buying a $35.50 CSL call option as you think the market cost of CSL will rise significantly in the next two months. The current market rate of CSL is likewise $35.50.

These options are at-the-money; the option premium includes time worth just. There is no intrinsic worth in at-the-money options.

Time value.

Time value is a little bit harder to understand than intrinsic worth. Time value is the quantity you are prepared to spend on the possibility that the market will move in your favor throughout the life of an option so that you will profit on your purchase.

Time value in options will differ with in-the-money, out-of-the-money, and at-the-money options since each situation provides different opportunities and possibilities of a boost in the intrinsic value of choice. This is typical, the time value is most significant on at-the-money options, as this presents a chance for constructing inherent value into the option if the market relocates the ideal direction.

The further the strike cost is from the market value of the underlying stock; the following elements influence the less time worth the option will have time value:

- Time to expiry
- Volatility
- Rates of interest
- Dividend payments
- Market expectations.
- Time to expiry

The most apparent aspect impacting the time worth of an option is time itself. As valued time represents the possibility of a market motion in your favor, it follows that the more time you have in which to attain this market motion, the higher the chance is of it occurring. Hence, the longer the period left on an option contract, the higher the time worth will be. As the time draws close to the expiry date on your option, the chance for the option to increase in value minimizes. Hence, the valued time of your option reduces. This decrease in time value over the life of an option is called time decay.

Time decay is not a direct variable. That is, the time worth consisted of within an option cost does not minimize at a constant rate. Time worth lowers at a faster rate as you get closer to the expiration date.

When picking the expiration month of your option, you need to weigh up the cost of the option (which will be higher with more time to expiration) with the time required for your technique to work in your favor.

Volatility is the variety and speed in which a rate relocations. When a rate relocations by a large quantity within a short area of time, said it is to volatility high.

A buyer is looking for an option the price of the hidden share to move by an enough quantity to make a revenue on the option. For that reason, it follows that the volatility, or the range and speed in which the underlying stock relocations, will impact the price of the option.

The higher the volatility of the hidden share, the greater the time value of the option. Consider an option that is currently out-of-the-money. If the hidden share cost usually relocates a large variety within a brief space of time, it is more likely that the option will move into the cash and develop a value for the purchaser. As valued time represents the possibility of the marketplace relocating your instructions, it follows that options over show greater volatility will consist of a higher time value.

Rates of interest

When you purchase a call option, you have the benefit of taking advantage of as you just require to pay a fraction of the cost of the underlying stock to be exposed to movements in the price of that stock. For this factor, when interest rates increase, call option premiums will also increase in value.

You are successfully delaying the sale of your underlying stock up until you exercise the option when you purchase a put option. Put another way; you are postponing the time at which you receive payment for the sale of your stock up until you exercise your option. You would have those funds to invest in other places if you sold your stock right away. When interest rates increase, put option premiums fall as this delay in getting funds now carries a higher chance expense.

A rise in interest rates will trigger the premium of call options to trigger the bonus and increase on put options to fall.

When a business states a dividend payable to shareholders, both it announces dividend payment date and an ex-dividend date. When trading options, it is the date that the ex-dividend is very important. The day that ex-dividend date on which all investors who own the appropriate class of shares at the end of trade on that day will be entitled to the dividend payment. The next day, the share price falls typically by an amount similar to the dividend amount, as anybody who purchases shares on that day dividend will not be entitled. The dividend will be paid to the owner of the shares on the ex-dividend date, despite whether they still own the shares on the payment date.

A lot of significant businesses reveal and pay dividends at a comparable time each year and frequently at relative quantities. They will likewise provide income updates and other details to permit financiers to approximate the timing and amount of prospective dividends.

When selecting and pricing options, it is, therefore, crucial to consider any upcoming dividend announcements or ex-dividend dates. If the shares underlying has an ex-dividend date throughout the life of an option, this will affect the intrinsic worth of the option, without the option holder has any rights to any dividends. For this factor, any anticipated dividend announcements will be constructed into the option premium.

Market expectations

Ultimately, it is the expectations of purchasers and sellers that figure out the marketplace value of options. This will be constructed into the rate of any option premiums if the sellers and purchasers have an expectation of a particular movement in the market rate of the hidden shares.

Pricing models

As we have already detailed in this chapter, numerous factors will affect the premium price of an option. You need to consider the strike rate, the cost and volatility of the underlying stock, the time delegated expiry, anticipated dividends, and rates of interest in determining the reasonable worth of an option. An option model pricing is a formula that combines all of these factors to compute a fair value for you.

If options are priced at a reasonable value in the market, option prices models are used by financiers and traders to help them to identify. It is essential to note that the 'reasonable value' calculated by a rates model might not be the current market cost or the price quoted on the market by market makers. You still require to match a ready seller and a willing purchaser to sell an option and buy.

You do not need to be a specialist on option pricing designs to use one. An understanding of how they work suffices to be able to use an option pricing model to estimate the fair value of an option.

The ASX offers a theoretical option cost calculator on its site that you can use to compute a reasonable value for an option. The calculator provide you also with estimates for all of the variables, including dividend and volatility, which you can change.

Some of the factors that affect an option cost are understood, consisting of the strike price, market value of the underlying stock, and the time to expiry. Other aspects, such as anticipated dividends, interest rate changes in specific the volatility of the underlying stock, require to be estimated to calculate a fair worth. The two financiers utilizing the same rates design might still compute a different reasonable value for the very same option if their assumptions about volatility and dividends are various.

Volatility Approximating

In estimating the underlying stock volatility, you require to consider both the historical volatility and the suggested volatility. Historical volatility uses the rate range of the underlying stock over a recent duration and measures the actual fluctuations over this period. If you are utilizing historical volatility, you are assuming that the underlying stock will continue to behave comparably over the life of the option. The current market value of options has been based on the marketplace, view of the anticipated volatility of an underlying stock over the life of options. This likely most will be based on historical volatility; other expectations will be built into this estimation. The worth intrinsic in the present market rate of the option is called suggested volatility.

Fair worth versus market worth

Based on your estimates of dividends, projection rate of interest, and volatility, you are able to use an option price calculator to determine what you feel is the reasonable worth for an option. You then require to choose if you wish to participate in an option deal at the current market value. You can execute a trading strategy to profit from this chance if you feel that an option is mispriced in the market.

In basic terms, if you examine that an option is misestimated (generally as the indicated volatility is too high), then techniques involving writing options may fit as you have evaluated that the option premiums are currently too high. Additionally, if you assess that an option is underestimated (the suggested volatility is too low), then strategies involving purchasing options will permit you to buy options you consider are priced listed below their reasonable value.

CHAPTER SIX

Ways to Buy, Sell Or Options Exercise

This chapter, we shall look at the mechanics of options trading, how to open a position, and how you can then close your employment opportunity if you want to. We will also look at how you sell options and the margin requirements that are connected to offering options.

Towards the end of this chapter, we go over the new documents requirements you require to finish to trade options with your broker and how this may impact the option strategies your broker will permit you to carry out with them. Our last subject is the makers of the market. We discuss what they do and who they are.

Opening a position

As we discussed in chapter 1, you need to define or select the four essential regards to your option before you can sell an option or buy. The four basic terms (strike rate, the expiration date, the underlying stock, and if you are trading a put option or a call option) is set by the exchange. For underlying each commodity, there will be a series of a variety of put and call options offered that have numerous strike costs and expiration dates. A list of the complete options is provided from the exchange and also from many brokers.

It is referred to as trade opening. Whenever you enter an options trade by either purchasing or selling an option. If you offered an option, it is a first sale, and if you bought an option, it is an opening purchase. Your option position, either as a seller or a purchaser, is described as an employment opportunity.

The overall variety of open contracts in a specific type of option is described as the interest open. The options by their code are listed, with a bid rate and an asking price. The bid cost is the cost at which someone wants to purchase this specific option, and the asking price is the cost at which somebody is willing to offer the option.

If you wish to purchase an option, you will put your order through your broker, just as you would buy a share. If you want to sell an option, you would likewise place your sale order through your broker.

You are able to place market and limit orders both for options. A market order is an order to sell or purchase at the best cost currently readily available on the market. A limit order is an order to sell or buy at a specific price only.

You might wish to continue to hold that position if you currently have an open area that is nearing its expiry date. It is possible to use a mix order to execute both of these trades in a single order. You can define the net cost at which you want to roll over your position, but you do not require to determine a cost for the leg of each trade. If the order goes through, the close of both the preliminary position and the opening of a new location will be carried out at the same time.

It is vital to note options orders all on the ASX are suitable for day orders. This means that any requests that have not been filled at the end of the trading day will be erased. If you still want to put your order the next day, you will require to place a new order in the early morning.

Closing a position

To close your option position, you just place an order to cancel out your employment opportunity. To narrow your option position, you would put an order to sell the same type and amount of the option contract if you had acquired an option.

Clearing Options

The clearing and settlement functions for the options market are entirely various from the market share. On the market share, all the trades are executed between a specific buyer and seller, and settlement of the business takes place three trading days later on. In Australia, the ASX does the functions of both solutions and trades.

Trading of Options on the ASX; however, a separate organization, ASX Clear, is accountable for the settlement function. This needs ASX Clear to both clear all options that are traded on the ASX and ensure that all contractual responsibilities associating with options are met. If an option holder wants to exercise their option, ASX Clear is accountable for ensuring that they designate this to an option seller and that the seller satisfies this obligation.

When you position an option order through your broker, your broker becomes your trading participant and is accountable for registering your trade with the ASX. When the trade is carried out, a contract is produced between your broker and the other celebration's broker. This contract is called the marketplace contract. At this point, a procedure of novation occurs in which the market agreement is changed by two separate agreements are as followed:

Between the broker and ASX contract Clear

A contract between the other celebration's broker and ASX Clear.

Under this procedure of novation, ASX Clear becomes the counterparty to all open option positions. As an option buyer, you do not require to evaluate the credit danger of the seller and their capability to satisfy their commitments if you decide to work out or sell your option.

Purchasing or selling an option develops an agreement between parties. Unlike when you are buying or offer shares, there is no transfer of ownership or title to the underlying shares.

Option settlement

As we have simply described, ASX Clear is accountable for the settlement of all OPTION contracts. Solution for options agreements occurs one service day after the trade date. This is typically described as T +1 (where T stands for transaction day). This is different from share deals, which pick the 3rd service day after the agreement and are referred to as T +3.

You need to pay your premium one service day after you purchase it if you buy an options contract. You will receive the incentive of one business day after you have sold it if you offer an option.

Exercise options

If you exercise or wish to buy your option, you require to notify your broker who is required to send a workout notice to ASX Clear. When ASX Clear receives a workout notice, it will arbitrarily choose an author who has sold the same type of OPTION and will designate the workout to the writer. It is far too late to liquidate your position as soon as ASX Clear has assigned a workout notice to an option you have offered.

When an option is worked out, the transaction is settled within three working days after the option is exercised; that is, T +3. This is in line with the stocks of settlement. This is a reason that the option's writer can purchase the underlying stock from the marketplace (which settles T 3) if they require to adhere to the workout of a call option, and they do not presently hold that stock. You will receive and pay for the underlying shares three service days after exercise if you exercise your call option. If you have offered a call option that is applied, you will receive payment for the shares at the strike rate and need to deliver the shares three service days after the exercise. Option agreements are settled T +1.

The workout of options are settled T +3. If you exercise or do not an in-the-money OPTION before the expiry date, it will end worthless, despite just how much intrinsic value might be attached to that options. To prevent this, you need to guarantee that you monitor your option positions and either offer or exercise your options before the date of expiry.

It is possible to set account for trading to auto-exercise so that your options will automatically be exercised if they are in-the-money at expiry. This is particularly helpful for cash-settled index options, as the workout of the options continually leads to a cash payment rather than the delivery of an underlying share.

Trading expenses

Payable Brokerage will be on any OPTION orders that are carried out. Brokerage rates will differ in between brokers and might be payable at a flat rate or as a percentage based upon the option premium, or a mix of both a flat rate and a portion. You will need to consult private brokers to identify the brokerage rates and structure that will best suit you. ASX Clear likewise charges a cost per contract, which may be included in your brokerage or may be charged to you separately by your broker. Youwill also pay an exercise fee if you want to exercise your OPTION.

Limits

When you write a contract of an OPTION, you have a prospective obligation to deliver the underlying shares if that OPTION is worked out. As an OPTION author, you may likewise have potentially limitless danger if the market moves versus your position. To ensure you can fulfill this obligation, ASX Clear requires all options writers to provide a margin.

Tip

If you offer an options agreement, you only need to supply a margin. Option buyers need not provide any margin for their employment opportunities.

ASX Clear determines the quantity of a security that it deems needed to ensure that the option's writer can meet their obligations under the options contract. As the options agreement worth is impacted by the market price of the underlying stock, the value of any margin requirement will also change as the market price of the underlying stock changes.

ASX Clear computes the margin requirements utilizing a system referred to as the ASX Margining DERIVATIVE System (ADMS). This marginal calculation of requirement using a set formula that considers the current option premium and the volatility of the hidden security.

The margin needed for options consists of two parts:

- **A margin premium**

The margin is the premium value of the premium connected to your OPTION at the close of every day. This is generally the quantity you would need to close out your option position by buying the same type of options.

The risk margin is developed to cover the possible motion in the premium margin on any given day. This is determined by the recommendation to the intraday movement of the price of the hidden share, and this movement is referred to as the daily volatility. This volatility is expressed as a portion and understood as the margin period. The ASX publishes and updates the margin for all OPTION classes each week.

Tip

Your margin requirement will be computed on your whole portfolio of open options agreements so that some positions might offset the margin requirements of other positions every day.

As you understand, because of the procedure of novation. ASX Clear has a broker contract with your option agreement, instead of with you straight. ASX Clear will enforce the margin on your broker, who will, in turn, require you to offer them with a margin for your option contract. You must know that your broker might examine your margin threat differently to ASX Clear and need a more significant margin than that calculated under ADMS.

As an OPTION seller, you will need to provide either cash or other security to cover your margin. The additional collateral generally includes shares you own or bank assurances. If you are offering shares as collateral, your broker might need more than your margin to guarantee versus any harmful falls in those share values.

Usually, your broker will establish a separate options account where they will hold your margin, including the premium you got on offering the options agreement. They will then move shares or money between your trading account, and your options account as required to cover your margin. When you close your options contract, and it has been settled, they will transfer the value of your options account back to your trading account.

When your margin boosts and you do not have the readily available funds in your trading account, you will get a margin call from your broker. This will need you to deposit extra funds or security to cover the margin within a set amount of time, usually 24 hours. If you are unable to or stop working to meet a margin call, your broker might close out your OPTION positions without further reference to you.

To purchase or write an option, you will need to open an account of an option with your broker. You will sign an Options if need Client Agreement, which remains in addition to the brokerage contract you require for a share trading account with your broker. As part of the processes of setting up an options trading, your broker needs to identify your suitability for this type of trading technique. It is most likely they will ask you to finish a questionnaire to assess whether options are an appropriate investment for you. You might be requested details about your financial investment experience, financial position, danger tolerance understanding of options, and your business goals in trading options. Your broker might limit the techniques you can trade through them based on your responses to those questions.

Market makers

The ASX will establish many original series of options that are available for traders and financiers to sell and purchase. However, there may not always be providing retail traders a bid and ask rate for every single individual option. Market makers are the banks that can provide quotes and offers on the market so that financiers and traders can purchase and sell options for which there is not a retail counterparty. Having market makers offer these bids and ask likewise helps with valuing an options position.

There not be a difference for you if you purchase from or sell to a market maker than if you are buying from or sell to a retail investor. In truth, you will not understand if your option trade is with a market maker or a retail investor.

Market makers are financial organizations that run as professional traders and generally trade a wide variety of monetary instruments. They get a cost from the ASX to provide the quote and ask rates for options. Required to meet the requirements on the variety of agreements provided, the spread between the bid and ask price, and the duration over which they offer these contracts. The range is the distinction between the quoted rate (price at which the market maker is ready to buy an option) and the asking cost (price at which the market maker wants to offer an option).

You need to think about the spread as an expense of your options method. Throughout this book, we describe options examples with the market value of the options being a particular cost. In reality, there will be a cost to buy the options and a rate to sell the options. The range between these rates will add to the price of any options method.

Tip: The spread is tight (less difference between the ask and bid prices), the better for you as a financier. A big spread means that it will cost you more to leave your position.

Market makers are not required to offer a market all day every day. There is no warranty that the option you want to trade will have a price and amount available to trade. Specific occasions, such as company statements, high volatility in the underlying stock, or low liquidity in the underlying stock, will affect when market makers supply their bid and ask quotes. If a quote is not readily available for the options you wish to trade, you can request a quote from the market maker through your broker. Even still, it is sensible to have a plan if the marketplace maker does not offer a quote for your option, especially if you require to close an open option position.

CHAPTER SEVEN

How To Pick Option Strategy

When selecting an option technique, in this chapter, we will look at the essential factors you require to consider. When share trading, you have chance to purchase the option , then sell or hold your position. With options, there are many more options, each with various risks and chances.

No matter the method you pick, your objective will be to either earn a profit or restrict a prospective loss. In pursuit of these objectives, as a buyer of options you seek to purchase your OPTION at the most affordable price possible, and after that offer it (or exercise it) at the highest price reasonable. As an options writer, you work directly against the buyers in seeking to offer your options at the highest cost possible, and after that, close them out at the most affordable price possible or see them end useless.

For any options trade, the motion in the OPTION premium while you hold it will identify if you earn a profit or loss. You, for that reason, should think about all the elements that will trigger a modification in your OPTION premium. These aspects include: Movement in the rate of the underlying stock (and all the factors that might affect this).

Time to expiration and time decay

Modifications in volatility.

This is share trading in contrast, where you only require to consider the motion in the cost of the stock. Time decay and modifications in volatility are distinct to trading options. Although the motion in the price of the underlying stock is the most significant element affecting most options, it is essential to consider the impact of time decay and any modifications in the volatility of the underlying stock cost when crafting your option trading strategy.

Pointer.

Even if the underlying stock price is in relocations in your direction, you can still make a loss due to the impact of time decay or an unforeseen modification in volatility.

Movement in price.

The most significant factor affecting the cost of your option is motions in the cost of the underlying stock. You need the view of formed how the market cost of the underlying stock move is going. Since the time limitations in trading options, you likewise need to form a view of the cost motion of the underlying stock over a particular time duration and match your options expiration to this frame time.

You can determine your view on the movement price of the underlying stock using fundamental analysis, technical analysis, or a mix of both. The technique used to form your opinion is not appropriate to choose your options technique, as long as you can hypothesize about the movement of rate within the restricted life of an OPTION.

The following general guidelines can be used about picking an OPTIONS method based on your view of the cost motion in the underlying stock:

If you are anticipating significant movement in the market cost of the underlying stock, purchasing options might be a suitable technique. If you are not expecting a substantial motion in the market rate of the underlying stock, writing options may be an ideal strategy.

The impact of time decay is the reason. For an option buyer, any favorable movement in the market price of the underlying stock needs to be large enough to offset the time decay experienced while holding the option. The change in the market price of the underlying stock requirements to be significant enough to put the option in-the-money (if it is not there already), and boost intrinsic value sufficient to offset the reduction in time worth.

You might consider composing options as a method if you are expecting that the rate of the underlying stock will stay within a limited cost range. Once again, time decay, the reason for this is. If the underlying stock rate remains reasonably static, there will be little change in the intrinsic worth and a decline in time value, triggering the cost of the options to fall. The revenue capacity for an option writer is always the premium got, so big price motions in their favor are not beneficial to OPTION authors as they do not affect the revenue made.

Tip.

Option writers are typically looking for time decay to minimize the value of the options they compose so that their options expire worthlessly. The options author then keeps the option premium as a revenue.

Time decay.

All options have a minimal life that is specified by the option expiry date. All options will go through time decay over the life of the opportunity, and this reduction in time value will increase as the OPTION approaches the expiry date.

Time works against options buyers as they are speculating on a considerable cost movement in the underlying stock to happen before the expiration date. Not just do option purchasers require to hypothesize on a price motion, this motion should take place before the expiration date.

Tip.

Your view on the timing of cost movement in the underlying stock will affect your option of the expiry month.

Time decay likewise works against OPTION buyers, as it lowers the value of an OPTION regardless of any other favorable movements in the price of the underlying stock. Any increase in the intrinsic worth of options will consistently be minimized by the time decay of the OPTION.

As an OPTION purchaser choosing an expiry month, you need to balance versus having sufficient time for the stock price to relocate your favor and the cost of this time. Longer-dated options have a more significant time worth and, as a result, will likewise have a more significant premium. The OPTION strategy success will be extremely reliant upon the time that you have to the options expiration date, and the quantity you spent for that time.

As an OPTION seller, you need to stabilize the additional premium you get for longer-dated options versus the increased possibility that the underlying stock price will move against you in this time, and you will incur losses over and above your option premium.

Volatility.

Volatility is the cost variety in which the underlying stock to move is expected. As discussed earlier in chapter 4 on pricing, the volatility of the underlying stock is an essential element determining the time value of an option. This will impact the time value and, therefore, the premium rate of an option if there is a significant change in volatility in the underlying stock.

If the volatility of the underlying stock lowers, this suggests that the price range in which the stock will move has been decreased. It then follows that the value of time of the option will drop as the stock is less likely to attain a rate motion that will lead to a profit for the buyer of an option.

Therefore, if you have an unforeseen increase in the volatility of the underlying stock rate, this will increase the time worth of the options.

You have been enjoying the price of a mining stock for a long time. It has been moving within a minimal range in the last couple of months and has been experiencing decreased volatility recently. You feel the stock is going to break out into a trending upward relocation, which will develop a significant increase in the volatility of the stock rate.

In thinking about buying options over this stock, you require to consider your view of a boost in the rate of the capital, and an increase in the volatility of the stock rate. The motion in the stock price will impact the cost of the option the impact of this motion on your option price will depend on the kind of OPTION you purchase and the present market value of the stock concerning the strike rate of the options (that is, in-the-money it is).

The volatility in a change of the underlying stock cost will cause an increase to the options premium if this change has not been prepared for by the market and priced into the options already.

If you determine that a stock rate will experience a boost in cost volatility, a strategy involving buying options is likely to be beneficial as this will lead to an increase in time worth of your OPTION. If the stock price determined will experience a reduction in volatility, this will benefit an option writer by reducing the worth of the OPTIONs.

CHAPTER EIGHT

Techniques For Buying Call Options

In this chapter, we will talk about some general qualities, risks, and advantages included explicitly in techniques for purchasing call options. Usually, buyers of call options have a bullish view about the marketplace cost of a specific stock and are looking to benefit from this predicted increase in market price.

The most well-known technique for buying call options is speculating on a boost in the market worth of the underlying stock. It is an essential strategy that is more popular than purchasing put options, as it is more easily comprehended. In this chapter, we take a look at the thoughtful approach along with a variety of other less popular techniques, including purchasing call options.

Purchasing call options.

When buying call options, you are hypothesizing that the rate of the underlying stock will increase by a substantial amount within the restricted time duration to produce a revenue. The percentage returns on your trade if you are proven proper are enormous. If you are incorrect, you can lose some or all of the premium initial you paid.

Buying the right to you are to purchase 100 shares of the underlying stock at the strike cost at any time before the expiry date. You pay a premium for this right. Once you have bought your OPTION, you have three options:

- Sell your Options before expiry.

- Exercise your options before expiration.

- Allow the option to expire worthlessly.

As outlined earlier in chapter 6, the action you take will rely on the movement in the market rate of the hidden share, your expectation of any future motion before expiry, your factors for purchasing the call, and your danger tolerance.

Time is a substantial aspect of figuring out how you manage your options trade. Everyday options that you hold, the value time of your option will decrease. And it will reduce at an increasing rate as you approach the expiration date. In truth, even if the market price of the underlying stock increases before expiry, you might still lose cash on your OPTION due to the impact of time decay, counteracting any increase in intrinsic value.

Tip: The most significant problem for call option buyers is the lack of time and declining time worth in their options. Typically the market value of the underlying stock will increase over the life of the OPTION; however, it may not increase by enough to offset the decline in time worth. As a result, the buyer of the call option does not earn earnings on their investment.

Methods for purchasing call options

When the price of the WPL market was $40.00, you chose to buy a $40.00 WPL call option for $3.50. By the expiration date, the cost of WPL risen had to $42.00; however, your call option was now only worth $2.00.

How can you have money lost on your OPTION when the market cost of the underlying stock has risen?

When you bought your OPTION, it was at-the-money. As a result, the overall option premium of $3.50 consisted of time worth. Even though the stock cost increased by $2.00 and the intrinsic worth of your option increased by $2.00, this was offset by time decay of $3.50.

- Increase in intrinsic value$ 2.00.
- Decline in time value($ 3.50).
- Your net loss on the options *($ 1.50).

This estimation does not consist of deal costs. The above example shows that to earn a profit on buying a call OPTION, the marketplace worth of the underlying stock requirements to increase by enough to both:

- Balanced out the time decay.
- Create development in the intrinsic value of the OPTION.

There are several factors why you may think about buying call options as your trading technique. These include the following:

- Gain use
- Limitation your threat
- Hold-up a stock purchase
- Hypothesize for revenue.

Method 1: gain use.

Purchasing call options supply you with the benefit of taking advantage of. You need only to provide a fraction of the capital to purchase call options compared to buying the stock outright. This allows you to magnify your portion returns if you are proven proper.

Method 2: limit your danger.

Getting call options, instead of acquiring the stock directly, also allows you to limit your losses if the stock cost falls. You might wish to speculate on a boost in the market worth of a specific stock; however, you might also not want to be exposed to prospective losses if the marketplace value falls considerably. If the stock you purchase, you are exposed to the full quantity of any fall in the stock cost. With call options, nevertheless, you can just ever lose the premium you paid, despite how far the stock rate might fall.

Method 3: postpone a stock purchase.

When you purchase a call option, you are purchasing the right to buy 100 shares of the underlying stock at the strike price anytime on or before the expiry date. Therefore, you are securing the rate you will pay for the shares if you decide to work out the OPTION and buy the stock before the expiry date of the options.

You may want to invest long term in a specific stock as you feel it will increase in worth; nevertheless, for some factor, you wish to delay your purchase. Or perhaps you want to buy the stock however wishes to see it increase in worth first to confirm your analysis of an anticipated price boost. Buying a call option permits you to postpone your purchase but still lock in the price at which you will acquire the stock. The marketplace has experienced some substantial falls in value recently, and you wish to take advantage of the price depressed. There is a stock single you have been watching that, before the fall, was trading over $30 per share and is now trading at merely $18 per share. You think that the cost will rebound; however, you do not have the funds offered at this time.

You choose to buy a $19 call OPTION that has five months to expiry. The premium is $1. This purchase provides you the option to acquire the stock at $19 per share whenever in the next five months. You have five months to raise funds to purchase the shares and still purchase them at $19. Based upon what the stock rate does over this time, you can choose to offer your call options or exercise your call options and buy the stock at $19.

Method 4: hypothesize for profit.

A significant factor for buying call options is hypothesizing to generate short-term revenue. You are just speculating on the cost of the underlying stock rising by enough total up to make earnings on your options. You are not acquiring the call options with any intent to exercise them.

Time decay will trigger the worth of the call option to fall as long as you are holding the Option. For this factor, you need to be mindful of how you select the call options you wish to trade. You will require to stabilize the time you need for the stock to move in your instructions against the time value (expense) in the options premium.

You likewise require to consider the strike price concerning the current market price of the stock underlying. You need options to be in-the-money to produce a boost in intrinsic worth. Call options will be more affordable when they are out-of-the-money, as more extensive price motion is needed to generate inherent value in the option.

Conditions you should search for in selecting a call OPTION for speculation consist of:

The strike price need to be close to the current market value of the stock. When they are in-the-money options, this will ensure that the boost in the underlying stock cost will be shown in the price of your option.

The expiry time must be extended enough for your stock cost to increase adequately to balance out the time decay and create a profit on your call options.

Options with a low time value in the premium will lower.

The time decay, your options will sustain. As value time is the worth of the possibility of your options producing a revenue, call options will have a low time value if the market perception is that the underlying stock cost will remain steady or reduction.

You have been watching a mining stock just recently whose share price has been quite flat for a long time at around $25.00. Based upon your analysis, you believe the stock price will break out of its existing price range and move considerably upward by a minimum of $4.00 within a few weeks.

You choose to purchase 40 $26.00 call options for $0.10. These call options are low-cost as they are out-of-the-money, and the marketplace expectation for the stock is to remain flat. You only wish to run the risk of a little quantity to have the ability to take advantage of this possible relocation.

You will have a premium of the loss you paid of $400.00 if the stock does not increase above $26.10. If the stock cost does increase to $29.00, as you expect, you will make a profit of $15600.00.

There are some risks and downsides to acquiring call options that you require to be familiar with. Three primary dangers you need to consider are the time to expiration, time decay, and a fall in the volatility of the underlying stock cost.

Time to expiry

You are playing versus time, the value of the underlying stock requirements to increase by an adequate amount before the expiry date for you to earn a profit on buying options call. Your risk is that the stock underlying will stagnate in your favor before the expiry date, and you will lose some or all of your option premium.

Time decay

You likewise lose time worth on your options for each day that you hold them. The rate at which you lose time worth also increases the closer you move towards the expiration date. So you need a more significant rise in the price of the underlying stock to offset the time decay the closer you get to the expiration date. This requires to be factored into any options to continue holding your options as you approach the expiry date.

Idea: You may be appropriate in hypothesizing on a price rise; however, you may not earn a profit on your options if this rise is not big sufficient or doesn't occur before the expiry date of your options.

You must comprehend the pricing of the underlying stock and how this will impact the worth of your option at expiry. In particular, you require to be knowledgeable about the strike price and when your option will be in-the-money so that it has some intrinsic value. You should likewise understand the rate that the underlying stock needs to grab you to recuperate the option premium you paid and recover the cost on your trade. This will allow you to analyze the cost movement required before expiration for any call options you are considering to buy. You can then identify which strike cost and the expiration date is most proper for your call option method.

Idea: A pay-off diagram is an excellent tool for you to easily see the rate that the underlying stock should reach for you to offset the time decay over the life of the option.

Fall in the volatility of the underlying stock rate

As we went over in chapter 4, the time worth of your call option is based upon the implied volatility of the underlying stock cost. If the underlying stock rate experiences a decline in volatility, this will lead to a reduction in the value of your options. The factor for this is that when the underlying stock cost is experiencing a smaller sized variety of movement, the potential to profit on your call options is lowered.

You need to choose which call option you wish to purchase as soon as you have decided on your call options technique and the underlying stock. There will be options of a variety available with different strike costs, different premiums, and various expiration dates.

So how do you choose which are the most beautiful call options to purchase? The factors you need to consider in choosing your option consist of the:

- Strike rate concerning the current market value expiry date
- The volatility of the underlying stock cost

- Options premium.

Strike cost about the present market worth

Where the price strike is in relation to the market's current worth of the underlying stock will determine how far the underlying stock. Cost requires to increase to produce some intrinsic value (be at-the-money) and then how far above this rate you will recover cost and begin to earn a profit.

Depending on your view upon the stock underlying, you need to pick a call option with a strike rate that satisfies three conditions. You believe that the marketplace worth of the underlying stock will:

Methods for purchasing call options

Increase above the strike rate so that your options have intrinsic worth (unless you purchase in-the-money options).

Boost sufficiently above the at-the-money worth to balance out the premium you spent for the OPTION. Increase even further to develop an adequate return on your investment.

Expiration date.

The expiry date determinant is a key to whether your option method achieves success. You need the market worth of the stock to satisfy the above three conditions before they expire option. Assessing the frame time in which a stock will move needs to be based upon your analysis of the stock and is typically a harsh assessment.

If the cost of this stock will move adequately within your time frame to create earnings on your call options, the volatility of the underlying stock price will figure out. A stock with low volatility experiences just a small modification in cost and will not be likely to produce earnings for a call options buyer unless the volatility increases.

OPTION premium.

The cost of your options, or the option premium, will straight affect the earnings or loss you make on your option trade. Some basic standards selecting your OPTION you can use the following:

- A call option will strike lower the price:
- Require a smaller increase in the share rate to create revenue.
- Be more expensive than a similar outdated OPTION with a higher strike cost.

A call OPTION with a more extended expiry date will:

Give you a higher possibility of achieving earnings on your call OPTION as you have more time for the underlying stock price to move adequately in your favor.

Be expensive more than a call option with a much expiry date shorter.

Buying an out-of-the-money consistent call option is with a bullish view of the underlying stock as you require a significant increase in price to generate revenue on your call options.

Buying an in-the-money call option or an at-the-money is a less bullish view; however, it still requires an increase in the value of the underlying stock cost above the time value in the call OPTION.

Your challenge in choosing a call OPTION is to:

- Determine how far you think the underlying stock price will increase.
- Identify how long you think it will require to increase to that cost.
- Find call options that have a price strike and date expiry that fit with your analysis.
- Calculate your break-even point based upon premiums offered.
- Find the least expensive options that satisfy your requirements above and will produce a sufficient ROI.

CHAPTER NINE

Strategies For Buying Put Options

In this chapter, we are to move from a bullish market view to a bearish outlook and will concentrate on how you can use put options to make money from a falling stock rate. Provided as you are buying put options gives the right to sell your stock at a set price, you can lock in a selling cost in a falling market to either make money from this move or secure existing positions.

The standard method for investing in the stock exchange is to buy in a rising market and to remain out of a falling market. Put options, however, provide you a chance to benefit from a falling market. The value of an in-the-money put options increases as the price of the underlying stock falls. The more the fall in the market, the more your put option increases in value.

Purchasing put options can also assist you in securing earnings in your stock existing holdings. You can lock in a selling price (price strike on your put options) so that if the worth of your stock falls, it will be balanced out by a boost in the value of your put options. This resembles buying insurance for your stocks against a rate drop. All you lose is the premium put option you paid if the cost doesn't fall.

Buying put options

Buying a put option provides you the right to offer a stock at the strike cost at any time before it ends. Even if the market rate of the underlying stock has fallen below the strike rate, if you exercise your put option, you can offer your inventory at the higher strike rate.

Buying put options is a method you can use if you are expecting a fall in market value. As with all options, you pay for your premium put options. You may lose some or all of the premium you paid for the put options if the underlying stock rate does not fall.

It is not required for you to own the underlying stock to buy put options. You are still able to make money from a falling market by merely buying and selling the put options. Remember, as a buyer, you can offer the underlying stock, not the responsibility to sell. There are 3 OPTION strategies you can take after purchasing put options.

- Sell your option before it ends.
- Exercise your OPTION before it ends.
- Allow the options to end useless.

As we talked about in chapter 6, the strategy you take will rely on the factors you acquired the put options, the motion in the price of the underlying stock, your expectations of any more movements in this price, and your risk tolerance. Your options are limited to offering your OPTION or permitting it to expire worthless if you do not own the underlying stock.

You do not require to own the underlying stock to purchase put options. Time is a substantial aspect when buying put options, only as it is when purchasing call options. When buying a put OPTION to generate revenue, you require to think about the limitations of time to expiration and time decay.

Even if the marketplace worth of the underlying stock tips over the life of put options, if this fall is not substantial enough to cover the loss of time value, you will not benefit from your financial investment.

There are four main reasons for purchasing put options:

- Gain take advantage of
- Limitation your threat
- Safeguard your current long position
- Hypothesize for revenue.

These strategies operate in the very same way for call options other than that the value of your put options increases as the market worth of the underlying stock falls below the strike price of the option. In this chapter, we will cover only the points that are particularly pertinent for put options under each method.

Strategy 1: gain use

Buying put options to benefit from a falling share price is as essential as buying call options. You have a restricted threat and have the advantage of taking advantage of compared with short selling the stock.

Short selling is an approach of selling a stock on the marketplace and then repurchasing it later on. This is a strategy used to make money from a falling market as you sell now at the current market value, with the expectation of purchasing the stock back later at a lower rate. There are considerable limitations on brief selling shares enforced by both the stock market and brokers, plus not all brokers offer this service to all financiers.

Short selling is the opposite deal to buying shares straight as you offer the shares initially and then repurchase them at a later date. Your goal is to benefit from a fall in the share rate.

Offer stock Expectation Buy stock:

- At the current future
- Market value will fall

Buy stock Expectation Sell stock

- At current At future
- Market value will rise

In the very same method, as you have the advantage of leverage when buying call options, you likewise get the benefits of taking advantage of purchasing put options. You can acquire a reasonably sizeable direct exposure to the share rate movement for only a fraction of the expense. The percentage fall in the stock underlying will result in a considerably more massive percentage boost in your put OPTION value if your put option is in-the-money.

Strategy 2: limit your risk.

Utilizing put options enables you to speculate on a fall in the marketplace rate with restricted danger. When purchasing put options, the most you can ever lose on your deal is the overall premium you spent on the options. On the other hand, if you were to brief offer a share, your losses would amount to the value of any increase in the price of that share up until you close your position, despite how much the share rate might increase.

Strategy 3: safeguard your current long position.

There will be times when you think these shares may fall in worth if you hold shares. Many financiers react to this circumstance is one of 2 way:

The shares sell.

I hope the price and ride out the fall recuperates.

The smart investor has a third option. Buying put options provide you the capability to safeguard the overall value of your shares without the requirement to sell them.

There may be several factors you do not want to sell your shares, although you think that there is going to be a correction in the market cost of those shares. These reasons may include the following:

- You might not want to sustain the transaction costs of selling and later on buying the shares.
- You might not wish to lose your privilege to the dividend earnings shares on those.

- You may not wish a tax liability to incur on the sale.

Like all other traders, you can not be 100 percent sure that there will be a fall or be precisely sure when it will take place.

Purchasing put options conquers a lot of these issues. When purchasing put options, you do not need to sell your shares, so you keep your entitlement to any dividends that might be stated. You do not sustain a tax liability on sale, and if the share price goes up, you will still gain from this price increase.

Buying put options to secure an existing position is a hedging technique and a bit like buying insurance for your shares. You are securing an asking price for your shares. Any falls in the marketplace worth of your shares will be offset versus a boost in the value of your put options. No matter how far the share rate drops, your shareholding is safeguarded at the strike rate.

If the price of the hidden shares falls, you still have three OPTION courses of action offered to you.

You can keep your shares, offer your options, and understand a profit to offset the fall in your worth shares.

You can exercise options and sell your shares at the exercise price.

You can wait up until closer to the expiry date to determine your course of action.

Your hedging technique is guaranteeing versus a possible risk. Nevertheless, if this threat does not eventuate and your shares increase in worth, you benefit still from this increase. This would not be the case if you sold your stocks buying instead of options put.

You need now to assessing if you continue to wish to hedge against a prospective fall in the share price by rolling over your put options into another put option position, or you might have.

Modified your analysis and no longer want to enter into another hedging technique. For example, 10.4, we use the very same scenario as in the previous case but take a look at the benefit of this method when the share rate increases.

You presently hold 2000 NAB shares. You feel that the market stock is bearishly looking and desire to secure your NAB holding against an anticipated fall in value. NAB is presently trading at $25.00 per share.

You are prepared to fall covered in NAB of $1.00 to minimize the cost of protecting an even higher fall. So you decide to buy 20 $24.00 NAB put options for $0.70 so that you can safeguard the value of your NAB shares if the rate falls listed below $24.00. These options have three months to expiry. Three months later, the share price of NAB has, in truth, continued to rise and is now $26.00. Your put options are still worthless are out-of-the-money.

- Preliminary investment 20 options
- 2 000 shares.
- The system costs $ 0.70$ 25.00
- Expense$ 1 400.00$ 50 000.00.
- Current cost$ 0.00$ 26.00.
- Current worth$ 0.00$ 52 000.00.

Net revenue/(loss) *($ 1 400.00)$ 2 000.00.

* Net profit does not account for deal expenses.

If you decide to sell your NAB shares in anticipation of a fall in worth, instead of purchasing the put options as insurance coverage, you would not have gained from the increase in value of your NAB shares.

For example, your put options you have cost $1400; however, your shares have increased in value by $2000, so even though you were hedging against a potential fall in the market value of NAB, you were still able to gain from the resulting boost.

Once again, you now require to assess if you wish to continue to hedge against a prospective fall in the share price by rolling over your put OPTION into another put options position. Perhaps you still feel that the marketplace will fall, and you were too early, or possibly you have modified your analysis and no longer want to enter into another hedging strategy.

When picking a put OPTION to safeguard your present position, the options will come down to just how much you are ready to pay for the options and for how long you want the security for. Options that offer a greater level of protection (a higher strike price) over a longer duration (later expiration date) will have higher premiums.

Strategy 4: hypothesize for earnings.

Purchasing put options is a popular trading technique for creating a benefit from a falling stock cost. You are hypothesizing on the price of the underlying stock falling by enough amount to cover your OPTION premium and generate a boost in the intrinsic worth of the put options. In this strategy, you need not to hold the stock underlying as you have no intention of working out the OPTION. Your method is to buy the put OPTION and sell it for revenue before it ends.

The conditions you must try to find in picking put options for short-term revenue are the same that we looked at for choosing a call OPTION for short-term earnings.

The strike price ought to be close to the current market price of the stock.

The time to expiry must suffice.

Options with low time worth in the premium will have less time decay; however, they are also less most likely to produce earnings. The risks and disadvantages of buying put options resemble purchase call options.

- Danger always limited to the premium you paid
- Minimal time to expiry
- Time decay.

- Fall in volatility.

Other techniques for benefiting from a falling stock cost consist of short selling and selling call options. However, the risk profile for these methods is hugely different. Short selling and selling call options expose you to endless danger.

Pick your put option.

In choosing your put OPTION, it is insufficient to correctly forecast that the marketplace value of the underlying stock will fall. You are hypothesizing on a significant sufficient motion to happen within the life-limited of your OPTION. Even if correctly you pick the downward movement within your amount of time, this will be offset by the reduction in time worth of your options.

Low options priced that are out-of-the-money have a lower danger and time value and will need a much bigger movement in the cost of the underlying stock to produce any amount intrinsically. The efficient market is in re-pricing options to represent market expectations, time to expiry, and the movement in the price of the underlying stock. Low priced options are low-cost for a factor. There is little time value in the options as there is only a small opportunity that the options will produce any intrinsic worth before they end. If you purchase an in-the-money put option, any movement in the underlying stock rate to the disadvantage will develop a dollar for dollar revenue in your put OPTION (less time decay). However, any boost in the market value of the underlying stock will likewise directly minimize the worth of your put options as long as it remains in-the-money.

It is erroneous to think that inexpensive options are always deals. Cheap options are out-of-the-money and most likely to expire worthlessly.

You require to think about the very same factors in selecting your put options as you consider when choosing a call option. These elements include the following:

- Strike price with the present market worth
- Expiration date.
- The volatility of the underlying stock price
- Option premium.

Some general standards you can use in picking your put option are as follows:

Put options with a higher strike cost will need a smaller sized fall in the share rate to produce a profit be more costly than a similar dated option with a lower strike price.

A put OPTION with a more extended expiry date will provide you a higher opportunity of attaining earnings on your put option as you have more time for the underlying stock rate to move adequately in your favor.

Be expensive more than a put OPTION with a much shorter expiration date as it has a higher time value.

Buying an out-of-the-money put option consistent is with a bearish view of the underlying stock as you need a substantial reduction in cost to produce a profit on your put options.

In-the-money put option Buying, or an at-the-money is a less bearish view, but still requires a fall in worth of the underlying stock cost over and above the time worth in the put options.

Your challenge selecting in a put option is to determine how far you believe the underlying stock cost will fall.

Figure out the length of time you think it will require to fall to that cost.

Discover put options that have a strike rate and expiration date that fit with your analysis. Compute your break-even point based upon premiums offered. Discover the least expensive options that meet the requirements laid out above and will create enough return on investment.

CHAPTER TEN

Strategies for selling covered call options

Selling call options can be a high threat or quite conservative, depending upon whether you own the underlying stock or not and how you structure your trade. If you offer call options and you own the underlying stock, you are offering covered call options. This is a conservative method with a limited threat. If you call prospects to sell and you own not the underlying stock, you are selling exposed or naked call options. This is a high danger strategy with potentially unlimited risk.

In this chapter, we will go over the general qualities, advantages, and drawbacks of offering covered call options. We will also talk about several techniques that can be used and the threats attached to these strategies.

Offering covered call options is a technique in which you can earn an income in the kind of option premiums got. This is especially effective as a technique when stock rates stay flat or within a narrow trading range. This method allows you to generate extra earnings from your stock position without relying on capital growth.

It is crucial to evaluate if this method is suitable for you and your investment goals if thinking about offering covered call options. This includes establishing an understanding of how to carry out a call selling strategy and the risks involved and having a proper level of experience in the stock exchange.

Offering call options

When offering call options, you reverse the order of a typical investment or trading deal. You open your position by providing the opportunities first, and then one of the three strategies will take place:

- You can purchase the option back later on to close your area.
- The option expires useless so that you do not require to purchase it back at all.
- The options are worked out versus you.
- Buyback call options
- Offer call options end useless options
- Options are exercised versus the seller

Time is an advantage significant to call OPTION sellers. Just as time works against the buyer of an option, it works for the options

Techniques for offering covered call options seller:

For an OPTIONS seller to lose money through the sale of a call OPTION, the marketplace value of the underlying stock price should increase by an adequate total up to balance out both the time decay and produce a boost in the intrinsic value of the options. And this must be achieved within the minimal life of the OPTION before it expires.

Time on your side works well as a call options writer (seller).

An OPTION which contains a higher time value in the OPTION premium has higher potential earnings for the option seller.

 The higher the time decay in options, the much better it is for the OPTION seller.

As an author (seller) of covered call options for income, you are hoping that the worth of the underlying stock will stay constant and below the strike price of the options. In this circumstance, the option will have no intrinsic value and will not be exercised. The worth of your underlying stock will likewise stay steady and not lose value. If the marketplace worth of the underlying stock remains below the strike cost to expiration, the options will end useless, and you, the writer, will retain the OPTION premium as revenue.

As an options writer, your earnings are mostly the decreasing time value that the purchaser experiences over the life of the options.

When you call the option to sell, you are approving the purchaser of the option the right to purchase 100 shares of the underlying stock at the strike price at any time before the option expires. This implies that you are handling this responsibility, and assume the danger of being needed to provide those 100 shares in the event that your OPTION is exercised.

As an OPTIONS writer, you have no control over if or when your options may be worked out. This is the purchaser; if your call is out-of-the-money so that the market worth of the shares is below the strike price, then your request will not be exercised. Your danger ends up being evident when the market worth of the underlying stock moves above the strike cost of the OPTION.

It is essential to note that as a call options author, you do not commit to keeping your option position open to expiry. You can close your options position at any time before expiration by buying back the same option.

There are several possible results for an OPTIONS writer. The actions you might take as an options author will depend upon how the worth of your OPTION changes and what your expectations are for the time staying on the options.

If your call options out-of-the-money, you can remain either:

Hold to your expiry call options, at which time they will expire uselessly, and you will keep the OPTION premium as an earnings

Close your option position at a time by purchasing back the options at their current market price.

If the marketplace value of the underlying stock relocations above the strike rate and your call options move into the cash, you are at risk of having your options worked out at any time. At this moment, the following options are readily available: You can continue to hold the open options position.

You may enjoy selling your stock at the strike rate, or you may feel the price will fall, and you choose to run the risk of the options being exercised to see the possibilities return out-of-the-money.

Your OPTION position can be closed at any time by redeeming the options at their current market price.

Your position can be rolled to a new OPTION with a higher strike cost and later expiry date. This includes the time buying back your employment opportunity and selling a new one.

They will most likely be worked out, and you will be obliged to deliver the underlying stock at the strike price if your options are in-the-money at expiration. When selling call options, it is crucial to understand the threats and prospects for loss to handle your position effectively.

Selling covered call options

As a stock financier, you will experience the number of times throughout which the price of your shares remains flat, or within a narrow trading variety. This time, you will experience not any growth on your financial investment, and the only gains you will get will be from any dividends paid during that time. If you think that your shares are not likely to move significantly, the majority of investors would simply examine one of two options:

- Hold your stocks to get any dividends to be paid and hope that the shares will ultimately increase in worth.
- Invest your capital and sell shares in other shares or financial investments that are likely to produce a much better return.

However, selling covered call options offers you the third course of action that will enable you to earn earnings from your financial investment even when the worth of your shares is not increasing.

When composing covered call options, your options are 'covered' by the underlying stock that you currently hold. In producing hidden call options, you are approving the right to the purchaser to purchase your underlying stock at the strike price. To guarantee that you satisfy this obligation in the occasion of your options being worked out, required are lodge your stock to ASX Clear. (Your broker on your behalf will do this.) If your choices are worked out, ASX Clear will provide the shares to the counterparty that worked out the options and forward it into account at the purchased rate.

While your lodged shares are as security for your covered calls, you are unable to sell them. You do, however, still maintain ownership of the stock (unless your option is worked out) and will receive any dividend privileges that develop during that time.

If you are thinking about selling covered calls, you need to think about the following:

You ought to expect that the market rate of your underlying shares will stay flat or may fall.

A decrease in the volatility of the marketplace cost of the underlying stock will be advantageous to you.

If the market rate of the underlying shares boosts above the strike rate, you may be bound to offer your shares at the strike price, which would be below the current market value.

If your shares increase significantly in worth, your profit potential is restricted even.

Following are three essential techniques when writing covered calls you can use:

- Provide income as a source from the premium OPTION.
- If your view is that the marketplace rate of your stock is most likely to stay flat or within a consistent trading range.
- Selling call options over this stock can offer you with income from the option premium when your shares are not producing any capital gains.

Methods for selling covered call options

Provide some protection from a fall in worth stock of you.

If you are concerned that the value of the shares might fall, however, do not wish to sell them at present.

Writing covered calls over those shares will supply earnings that can be offset versus the fall in worth, thus providing you with some downside security and limiting your total loss.

Potentially sell your shares above the marketplace worth. You can write a call option to offer your shares at the strike cost you are pleased to get. You get both the OPTION premium and the strike cost for your stocks if the market value of the underlying shares relocations above this price, and your options are exercised.

Technique 1: offer an income from the OPTION premium

To produce an income stream from selling covered calls, you must have the view that the market price of your underlying shares will stay flat, or at least listed below the strike rate of your options. This will permit you to keep the options premium as earnings when the options end useless, and the value of your underlying shares will stay stable.

The very best possible outcome when selling covered call options is when the market worth of the underlying stock is at or just listed below the strike rate of your call options. When this takes place, you will have two favorable results:

- Your shares have not fallen in worth.
- You keep the full OPTION premium.

Technique 2: supply some defense from a fall in the value of your stock.

When the market worth of your underlying stock is falling, will provide you with premium income that, selling covered calls, you can use to balance out the fall in the value of your stock.

You need to determine that the technique for holding your shares, even though you are anticipating them to fall, stands. This is frequently the case for a long term financial investment method and an expected short-term retracement in price.

Next, you need to identify just how much defense you wish to have and select your OPTION accordingly.

You own shares of 4000 WBC that are currently trading at $21.30. You are worried that the market is weak, and your shares are going to fall in worth; however, you desire to hold them for the longer term.

To acquire a higher level of security, you would need to offer a more top-priced call option. This an option would be that had a more extended expiry date (therefore a more significant time value) or a lower strike price.

Technique 3: potentially offer your shares above the market value.

To achieve a better price from offering covered calls, instead of selling your shares at your target rate, you provide a hidden call option that has a strike cost equal to your target price. Instead of getting your target rate on sale, you sell your shares at your target price and get your call option premium.

In this method, the most you will ever get for your shares is the strike cost plus the premium. You require to account for both the options and the hidden shares Whenever you determine your profit or loss on composing covered call options.

Dangers and disadvantages of offering covered call options:

There are a few dangers and disadvantages to selling covered call options that you require to be mindful of. The most considerable threat is that there may be a significant fall in the rate of your stock underlying. This loss will result in value on this stock that will only be partially balanced out by the OPTION premium you received.

As the stock holds as collateral for your call options, you are unable to sell this stock up until you close your option position or the option expires.

Another drawback of offering covered call options is that they restrict the revenue you can make on your underlying shares. If your analysis is inaccurate and the market cost of the underlying stock has a big unexpected boost putting your options in-the-money, your options may be exercised.

Upon workout, you would be required to offer your underlying shares at the strike price of the option, missing out on the increased value above the strike rate. This is referred to as a chance expense. It is not an understood loss that you incur, however a revenue (or chance) that you miss out on out on.

CHAPTER ELEVEN

You are taking a guaranteed premium income now to forgo a potential gain throughout the life of the options.

You are not obliged to hold your covered call options to expiry. If the marketplace rate of the underlying stock boosts towards the strike cost or relocations above the strike price, you may think about purchasing back your options at a loss. If you did not want this to happen, this would get rid of the danger that your options will be worked out.

Although it is most likely that your options will be exercised near to the expiry date, this is not always the case. You require to accept that it may be applied at any time if your option is in-the-money. You likewise need to be conscious of any ex-dividend dates, as your options will be most likely to be worked out if the underlying stock is about to go ex-dividend.

Suggestion: When your options move into the cash, you require to either accept the threat of exercise or redeem options to close your position.

Select your covered call options.

You need to choose on which call OPTION to write as soon as you have determined upon your covered call option technique and comprehend the risks included. For any stock, you will have a variety of exercise prices and expiration dates to select from.

The lower the strike price, the bigger the premium you will receive. This will offer you with higher earnings and more protection versus a downside relocation in the underlying stock. The lower strike rate also suggests that you will receive a lower price for your shares if the market value increases and your options are exercised.

Your option of strike price will depend on your view of the market worth of your underlying shares and your reasons for writing the covered calls. If you have an outlook bearish and are concerned about safeguarding your downside risk, a lower strike rate fits with this view. If your picture is more neutral and you wish to hold your stock, you will need to select a strike price that you think will keep your options out-of-the-money for the life of the option.

Techniques for offering covered call options:

Longer-dated options will have higher premiums, but they also increase the time over which the options may move into the cash and be exercised. Your danger here is that the underlying stock has a longer time in which to break out of its present trading range before the expiration date of your options. This will work versus your covered call technique if the stock cost moves unexpectedly either up or down.

You require to be prepared to have the options exercised Whenever you write a covered call option. There is always the threat of your option being used if the call is in-the-money. Up previously, all of our examples have involved selling calls covered that are out-of-the-money. However, this does preclude you not from selling calls in-the-money for short-term revenue. You do, however, comfortable need to be with the threat that your options might be worked out at any time that they remain in-the-money.

Your decision to offer your options has netted you a tidy short-term revenue in addition to offsetting the fall in the value of your underlying stock.

Following conditions are some for you to be aware of when picking your covered call OPTION:

The strike rate of the OPTION is higher than the original expense of your underlying shares. If the OPTION is exercised, this will ensure you make earnings on both your option and your shares.

The call is in-the-money, but not deep-in-the-money. This will mean that the options have intrinsic value that will move one to one with motions in the underlying stock price. This provides a chance to close your option position for short-term revenue.

The call is not deep but out-of-the-money out-of-the-money. This will indicate that the overall options premium is the time value, and the time value will be higher than if the option was deep out-of-the-money. As long as the underlying stock rate remains listed below the strike cost until expiry, you will keep the complete OPTION premium as revenue.

The time to expiry. The time to expiry requirements to be enough time to create time value in your option when you sell it, but not too long to decrease the threat of the options moving into the money.

The options premium. The premium you get for your OPTION needs to be large enough to compensate you for handling the risks of an option writer. When choosing your covered call option, you need to consider all of the lists below elements:

- Your technique for offering the call OPTION Ã the premium you will receive
- The mix of time worth and intrinsic value in the premium Ã time delegated expiry

Your expectation of motion in the price of the underlying stock in the time delegated expiry, the gap between the current market cost of the underlying stock, and the strike price of the options.

In managing your covered call position, you likewise require to consider your goals in holding the underlying stock in addition to your call options strategy. This will influence your options to close out an options position or to continue to keep it when it is approaching or is currently in-the-money

Techniques for offering naked call options

Selling naked call options, or exposed calls is a strategy where you offer call options but do not own the underlying stock. This is a high threat technique, as your losses are possibly unrestricted. Since of the high danger profile of offering naked call options, this technique is just recommended for traders who have enough experience and ability in the market to handle such a position.

In this chapter, we will discuss the benefits and disadvantages of offering naked call options and a few of the strategies that can be used.

Selling naked call options

When selling a naked call OPTION, you are giving the right to the purchaser to buy 100 shares of the underlying stock at the strike price. What occurs if your options move into the cash and are exercised?

Theoretically, you are needed to provide the stock to the option holder. You would need to purchase the stock at the dominating market price, and after that, offer it to the holder of the option at the price strike. This may result in a loss to the options seller, as the options will only be worked out if the market cost of the underlying stock is higher than the strike rate of the option. And this is where the limitless danger can be found in. As there is no theoretical limitation on how high the speed of the underlying stock can rise, there is no limitation on the losses you might incur.

The settlement time for working out an OPTION is T +3 (three days after a workout). This is to enable time for the purchase of the stock underlying(all stock settlements are T +3) if required.

This is the settlement contrast to period for buying and offering options, which is only T +1.

In practice, nevertheless, it is the settlement house, ASX Clear, that delivers the underlying stock on the exercise of options. You will remember from chapter 11 that when you offer covered call options, ASX Clear holds your stock to 'cover' your OPTION position. If the option is worked out, ASX Clear collects the sale follows the holder of the option and provides the shares to them. ASX Clear passes then on the proceeds to sell the OPTION writer.

For naked options call, upon exercise ASX Clear will buy the stock at the current market value to provide to the holder of the option who exercised the OPTION. ASX Clear would also gather the earnings on the sale of the stock at the strike cost As an options seller, and your account would be debited with the difference between the expense to acquire at the market worth and the sale proceeds at the strike cost.

When offering naked calls, you are needed to supply a margin that is held by ASX Clear. This margin is determined as the amount of security that ASX Clear deems required to guarantee that you can meet your responsibilities under the option agreement. This margin quantity will differ with the marketplace cost and volatility of price motions of the stock underlying. ASX takes the funds clear they require on the workout of an OPTION from your margin. Describe chapter 5 for more detail on margins.

The losses from selling the naked option call can be significant if there is a substantial boost in the market value of the underlying stock above the strike cost.

As talked about in chapter 11, essential attributes of offering either covered call options or naked call options are:

Time.

When selling option calls due to time decay, Time is a substantial benefit.

Control.

As the seller of options, you have no control over when or if your options will be exercised. This is the right of the OPTION purchaser. You do, nevertheless, have the option of closing your options position at any time before it is worked out and before expiration.

Option worth.

The most substantial elements that will affect the value of your OPTION are:

- Modifications in the market cost of the underlying stock.
- Modifications in the volatility of the market rate of the underlying stock

Time staying to expiry.

The most considerable difference between selling covered call options and offering naked call options is a threat. When selling covered call options and the marketplace moves versus your option position, you only sustain the opportunity expense of selling below market price. When selling a naked option call and the market moves versus you, your possible losses can be unrestricted and substantial.

Due to the involved risks, brokers will have specific requirements that you should satisfy to sell naked call options. These will consist of the level of equity in your account, and your experience in trading both options and equities.

Generally, you will be appointed an options trading level based on your experience, which will determine what types of methods you can use. Offering naked call options (and offering put options) will require a higher options trading level than buying options or offering covered call options.

When selling options call is when the market worth of the underlying stock is equivalent to the strike price of the options plus the OPTION premium, the break-even point. Therefore, it is still possible for an options writer to earn a profit on the sale of naked call options when they are exercised, as long as the marketplace worth of the underlying stock is less than the break-even price.

Workout of your option does not necessarily imply you lose on your OPTION trade. You just understand a loss if the market worth of the underlying stock is above your break-even point.

Naked call OPTION strategies.

When offering naked call options is to make earnings from your trade, your goal. To benefit from offering naked call options, you need among the following occasions to occur:

The underlying stock cost stays below the strike rate so that the OPTION wastes time to value and ends worthless. The underlying stock price falls so that the worth of the option reduces, and you can close your position at a profit. The underlying stock price increases, however, by a small adequate quantity so that the time decay on your option offsets any other increase in time or intrinsic worth.

When handling your naked call option position, you can either:

- Close your positioned option at any time before it is worked out and before it expires
- Hold your option position.
- To close your option position, you merely redeem the option at its current market value.

The method which you handle your open naked call option position will depend upon the movement in the price of the underlying stock and the subsequent effect on the market worth of your option.

There are four ways at which the market worth of the underlying stock can move:

- The value of the underlying stock falls
- The worth of the underlying stock stays constant.
- The worth of the underlying stock increases but remains below the strike rate of the option—the value of the underlying stock increases above the strike price of the options.
- The worth of the underlying stock falls.

When the market worth of the underlying stock falls, this is a piece of excellent news to the seller of a naked call option. The quality of the option will decrease due to time decay, and the possibility that the prospect will move into the cash is reduced.

You may want to close your option position at this time if you wish to realize revenue on your trade by purchasing back the option at a lower rate. You do this only if you would felt that the market worth of the stock underlying will reverse and might above move the price strike of the option. Now deep as the option is out-of-the-money, it is more likely that you would merely hold the option to expiry and see it end useless.

The value of the underlying stock remains constant when the marketplace worth of the underlying stock stays constant; the quality of the option will decrease due to time decay.

You may close or wish your option position at this time if you want to understand a profit on your trade by redeeming the option at a lower rate. As soon as once again, you would do this if you felt that the market value of the underlying stock might rebound.--and move above the strike rate of the options.

The worth of the underlying stock boosts but stays below the strike rate of the option when the market value of the underlying stock increases towards the strike cost of the option, the value of the option will alter in 2 aspects:

- It will increase due to a higher possibility of the option moving into the cash.
- It will reduce due to time decay.

The real modification in the worth of the option will rely on the interaction of these elements and might produce an increase, reduction, or no change in the value of the option.

You might want to close your option position at this time if you wish to avoid workout and are concerned about the increased danger of the market worth of the underlying stock continues to grow.

The worth of the underlying stock boosts above the strike price of the option

When the marketplace value of the underlying stock increases above the strike cost of the option, the option will be in-the-money, and workout is likely. The amount of the option will probably boost due to an increase in intrinsic worth.

You may want to close your option position at this time to prevent workout or additional losses due to the possibility of more considerable boosts in the value of the underlying stock rate.

As a seller of an option, you open your option position with a sale and close your option position with a purchase.

When selling naked call options, we will now consider a couple of strategies that you can use When handling any of these option techniques. You have the opportunity to close the position at any time (as we have merely detailed) based on the movement in the market value of the underlying stock.

Method 1: offering out-of-the-money naked call options.

When offering out-of-the-money naked call options, you are hypothesizing that the worth of the underlying stock will remain at or below the strike price of your option. If this happens, your call option will expire uselessly, and you will keep the option premium. This technique is described in WBC shares are trading currently at $21.30. You feel the price market is going to remain relatively constant and will not move over $22.50 in the next three months.

You choose to offer 40 covered call options for $0.50 with a strike cost of $22.50 and three months to expiry.

Over the next three months, the market value of WBC traded between $21.00 and $22.00 and was trading at $21.80 on the expiry date. The options expire worthlessly

- Option list price$ 0.50.
- Overall earnings on sale$ 2 000.00
- Option worth on expiry$ 0.00.
- Earnings on offering covered call options *$ 2 000.00.

Profit does not include deal expenses.

If, nevertheless, the market worth of the underlying stock boosts or you feel that the likelihood of an increase has become considerable, you can close your option position before expiry to understand a profit on your trade and prevent possible loss or workout.

Method 2: selling in-the-money naked call options.

Offering in-the-money naked call options is a risky and highly speculative strategy trading. As the options are in-the-money, they can be exercised at any time. You likewise face a one-to-one correlation between an increase in the market value of the stock and a boost in the intrinsic worth of your options.

This technique should be used only by traders experienced. When you believe it can be used, there will be an abrupt fall in the market worth of the share underlying. Any result that show fall is in an equivalent fall in the value of the options, which can then be closed at a revenue, or potentially expire useless if the market worth of the underlying stock falls.

Threats and disadvantages of offering naked call options:

The most substantial danger in selling naked call options is the capacity for endless losses if the marketplace value of the underlying stock boosts above the strike rate throughout the life of your option.

There are two other disadvantages to be mindful of: The requirement to offer a margin versus your open position is a significant downside associated with selling naked call options. If the market moves versus your call option and you will be needed to provide extra margin in the form of cash or securities, this margin will increase. Typically, you will be required to supply this within 24 hours.

Another essential drawback is that if you do suffer a loss on your option position and are unable to contribute extra funds to your account to cover the required margin, your broker might sell your securities existing to cover this loss. The sale of these securities may be poorly timed and not in line with your financial investment technique.

Due to the significant risk of possibly unrestricted loss from composing naked call options, it is essential to examine if this strategy is suitable for you. As we have stated, writing naked call options is a hazardous method, and you must consider the list below to consider identifying if it is a proper strategy for you.

Your danger profile. If the level of threat involved in selling naked call options is suitable for you, you require to assess. This needs to be examined because of your capability to manage a position with the potential for substantial losses, plus your financial capacity to sustain a worst-case circumstance. You do not want to erase your trading account from only one naked call option that moved all of a sudden.

Your understanding of the danger and of options:

It is imperative that you fully understand the risks involved and the specifications of the options you are considering composing. It is simple to end up being ecstatic about the potential for profit and downplay the prospective risks.

Your trading experience knowledge of a specific trading strategy is necessary; however, it does not change trading experience. Getting in such a high threat strategy, such as selling naked calls, needs you to have a reasonable level of expertise in the market. Your experience in the market will assist you in choosing appropriate call options, handling the inherent risk, and figuring out what level of threat you can handle, both emotionally and economically.

Your capital. When writing naked call options, you are needed to provide a margin to cover your position. Therefore the size of your trading account will determine the number and size of naked calls you can compose. You need to allow also additional capital in case of a margin call or adverse motion in the market worth of the hidden shares.

Your trading and financial investment objectives:

In crafting your total trading and investment goals, you will have broad goals about the types of trades you wish to get in, the level of threat you want to take, and the returns you want to produce. Composing naked call options may, if you are looking for high-risk, high yields, be appropriate for a portion of your overall portfolio. If you are looking for long-lasting, steady development, then other methods might be more suitable.

CHAPTER TWELVE

Strategies for offering put options

When you expect the worth of a hidden share to remain flat or increase a little, offering put options is a method you can use to benefit. Selling put options has the very same relationship to the worth of the hidden share as buying call options. The value of the invisible stock boosts, and so the earnings on your option position increases. The threat profile is different in this chapter, and we will take a look at the benefits and drawbacks of offering put options and likewise explore a few of the methods you can use when offering put options.

Selling put options.

When selling a put option, you are giving the purchaser the right to offer you 100 shares of the underlying stock at the strike rate. You receive a premium for accepting the threat that the option might be worked out, and you will be needed to buy the underlying stock at the strike cost.

As with selling a call option, when offering put options, your profit is restricted to the premium you get. If the market worth of the underlying stock is below the strike price of the option, the option will only be worked out by the purchaser. If your options are worked out, you are required to purchase the underlying stock at the strike rate, which will be higher than the present market worth of the capital. As a put option seller, you have control over not if or when your options might be worked out. You can, however, close your position option at any time before the option is exercised or expires.

The possible outcomes that you might deal with as a writer of put options are:

- Your option remains out-of-the-money and expires useless.
- You choose to close your option position before expiration.
- Your option moves into the cash and is worked out before expiration. This will need you to buy the underlying stock at the strike price.

Usually, the very best result for a put option seller is if the marketplace worth of the underlying stock stays above the strike cost of the option. This will lead to the option ending worthless, and, as the options seller, you keep the option premium as earnings.

You feel that the price of CBA hold is going above $50 over the next two months, so you decide to sell 10 $50 CBA put options for $1 when the marketplace price of CBA is $51.

By the expiration date, the price of CBA performed stay above $50. As the market worth of CBA never fell below $50, your put option was never in-the-money, so never at danger of being worked out.

At expiration, the put option is still out-of-the-money and expires useless. You maintain the $1000 premium as earnings on your option trade. This calculation does not include transaction expenses.

For example, the cost of the underlying stock moved in line with your expectations, and the option expired useless. In case 13.2, let's think about the scenario if the price of the underlying stock fell, contrary to your expectations.

Example.

You feel that the rate of CBA is going to hold above $50.00 over the next two months, so you decide to sell 10 $50.00 CBA put options for $1.00 when the market rate of CBA is $51.00.

In the next month, the cost of the CBA $48.50 is up. Your now options in-the-money and are priced at $2.00. What should you do?

For example, above, the marketplace worth of CBA has not moved in line with your expectations, and your options are now in-the-money. You have two options.

If the market worth of CBA continues to fall, Ö You can close your option position to mitigate the risk of the options being exercised or sustaining further losses. To narrow your position option, you would need to acquire the put options for $2, realizing a loss of $1000 on your trade (before deal costs).

Your other OPTION is to hold your option position. You would do this for one of 2 reasons. You might feel that the cost of CBA will rebound above $50 very quickly, and you are prepared to run the risk of workout in the short term to recoup the loss on your option position, possibly. The other factor is that you may feel that $50 is a fair cost for CBA, and you are happy to purchase the stock at this price. Your premium will offset the above market value you are paying so that the net cost of buying the shares is efficient $49.

Threats and downsides of selling put options

Selling put options brings the risk of considerable losses. Nevertheless, these losses do have a limitation, unlike offering naked call options. The worth of a put option increases as the worth of the underlying stock decreases. The maximum loss you can sustain is restricted to the strike cost of the option. If the market worth of the underlying stock fell to absolutely no, then your loss on the option would be the worth of the hidden shares at the strike cost, less the premium you got on selling the put option. Although it is unlikely to occur, this is your optimum risk exposure when selling put options.

You can alleviate the risk of loss through cautious options of stocks. It is not likely that a stock will trade below the company's net concrete possessions over the longer term (although it might fall below this in the short-term). When selling put options, referring to the net tangible ownership of the underlying stock gives you a reasonable basis in which to assess your threat.

Another element to consider requirements margins. When you sell options put, you are required to offer a margin to make sure that you can satisfy your responsibilities under the put option. This margin will increase considerably if your put option moves into the cash and is a threat of workout. You, therefore, require to have all set funds readily available to fulfill any margin calls.

The third threat you face is a workout.

You have the need to full capital required to acquire the underlying stock at the strike cost and commit this capital to purchase those shares if your put option is exercised. This can tie up your money in stocks which you now need to handle.

When selling naked call options, examining the risks of offering put options is a little various from your threat. With naked call options, you will realize a money loss if your options are worked out. When selling options put, you need to be prepared to purchase the stock underlying if your options are exercised. Although you can resell these shares on the marketplace right away, or whenever you pick, you need to be still prepared and able to acquire them entirely in case of exercise of your options.

There are methods in varieties you can apply when selling put options. The arrangements all depend on the expectation that the value of the underlying stock will remain consistent or boost in worth. We will talk about the following methods:

Supply an income source from the option premium utilizes your capital additional.

Shares purchase at a discount to your target rate.

Technique 1: supply an income source from the option premium

Hypothesizing on the rate of the underlying stock to create a short-term profit is the most popular reason for offering put options. To an income stream generated from selling put options, you should have the view that the marketplace price of the underlying shares will remain flat, and above the strike cost, you pick for your option. If the marketplace worth of the underlying shares does stay above the strike cost of your options, they will end useless, and you will retain the option premium as earnings. Consider this technique in WBC shares are currently trading at $21.80, and you are hypothesizing that the marketplace rate is going to stay reasonably constant and will not move below $21.00 in the next three months.

You choose to offer 40 put options for $0.50 with a strike cost of $20.50 and 3 months to expiry.

Over the next three months, the market worth of WBC traded between $21.00 and $22.00 and was trading at $21.50 on the expiry date.

The options expire uselessly

Option sale rate$ 0.50.

As your options were never in-the-money, (the marketplace worth of WBC never fell listed below the price strike of $20.50). For example, 13.3, there was never any possibility of your options being exercised. Your options ended useless, so as the option writer, you maintain the option premium of $2000.00.

The circumstance would be various if the market value of the underlying stock fell.

Example

WBC trading shares are currently at $21.80, and you are speculating that the market price is going to stay relatively constant and will not move below $21.00 in the next three months.

You decide to offer 40 put options for $0.50 with a strike cost of $20.50 and 3 months to expiry.

Over the next month, the marketplace worth of WBC fell to $20.00, and the put options are now worth $0.90. You choose to close your option position.

It is imperative whenever offering put options that you are prepared to purchase the underlying stock at the strike rate. For that reason, when selecting your put options, it is smart to choose stocks that you are comfortable owning at strike costs you feel represent reasonable value for those stocks. You can then manage your stock position appropriately.

This does not suggest that you want the options to be exercised, and might well select to close any open put option positions that are at threat of being worked out. It does indicate that you acknowledge that work out of your options is a threat of selling, and you are prepared to accept this threat and have a technique if the risk eventuates.

You have had success selling put options recent with no being exercised. You are feeling positive and have simply sold put options on five various securities to generate a considerable option premium.

In the area of a few days, an international occasion has caused a remarkable drop across the whole stock market, and all your put options fell under the cash and were exercised.

You now have to offer the capital to acquire all five stocks at prices above their existing market worth. You have to sell a few of your current stocks at a depressed value to satisfy your obligations under the put options.

Certainly, example 13.5 is a worst-case scenario. It is crucial to consider this result as a possible threat. In this example, you would have shares sold that you wished to keep at a reduced cost, to purchase stocks below their current market values. Your portfolio would be carry-ing a considerable unrealised loss, and you would have no free capital.

Method 2: utilise your extra capital.

This technique is based on your speculation that the market is misestimated and you do not wish to invest at present costs. Selling put options will enable you to create superior income, using your extra capital to fulfill the put options margins.

You will profit from the premium option if the stock rate continues to increase or stays above the strike rate. If the value of the stock underlying falls towards the strike price, you can either close your position or let the option relocation into the cash and buy the stock at the strike cost. In any case, you keep the option premium as a return on the capital you provided as a margin to sell your put options.

This technique operates in the same manner as method 1. The distinction is that this might be used as a short-term strategy for investors with spare capital who think the marketplace is overvalued, instead of an ongoing method of speculation for earnings.

Method 3: purchase shares at a discount rate to your target rate.

The 3rd technique in selling put options is to set your strike price at a target purchase rate to purchase the underlying stock at this cost. This is a method you can use if you wish to buy the underlying stock at a set cost that is listed below the current market price. The benefit of offering put options is that in addition to purchasing the stock at your target cost, you also get the option premium. Let's consider this, in example 13.6

You would like to purchase 500 WBC shares at $20.00. They are currently trading at $21.80. You decide to offer five put options for $1.80 with a strike rate of $20.00 and six months to expiry.

Over the next couple of months, the marketplace value of WBC is up to $19.50, and you get a notice that your options have been worked out.

Option price$ 1.80, Proceeds on sale$ 900.00 overall—purchase WBC at the 20.00 10 000.00 cost.

The net qualified expense to purchase WBC *$ 9 200.00. The current market price of WBC at 19.50 9 750.00

When the cost hit $20.00, for example, 13.6, you desired to buy WBC. So putting rather than in a limit order to purchase the shares directly, you sold a put option. This achieved your preferred result to buy the stock at your target rate and earned you an extra $900.00 in option premium. When utilizing this technique, there is the risk that your options may not be exercised. This risk is highlighted in the example below:

You wish to purchase 500 WBC shares at $20.00. They are presently trading at $21.80.

You choose to sell five put options for $1.80 with a strike cost of $20.00 and six months to expiry.

Over the next few months, the market worth of WBC fell to $20.10 to $22.00 increased.

Example: the disadvantage illustrates a bit of this technique. If the stock rate does not fall low enough for your options to be worked out, you might miss out on out on acquiring the stock. In selling your options put, you are required to supply capital as margin, so even if you chose to purchase the stock at above $20.00, you might not have the complimentary to do so in the capital. In that event, you would need to close your option position.

As a put seller option, you risk losing future revenues in the following two ways.

If the cost of the underlying stock increases, you lose the profits you might have gotten if you had merely directly bought the stock.

If the price of the stocks underlying falls drastically, If the option is exercised, are still needed to purchase the stock at the strike rate. You will be paying the market price above, and the sharp fall may alter your stock on this position.

In both cases these, you still retain the premium option as revenue. If your expectation is for the worth of an underlying share to remain steady or to rise somewhat, selling put options is a technique to generate a profit.

When selling option put, you are granting the purchaser the right to purchase the underlying stock at the strike cost any time before expiry.

If you are offering put options, you should be prepared to acquire the underlying stock at the strike price. This will guide you in your options of options.

Generally, the very best outcome for a put option seller is that the rate of the underlying stock stays above the strike price of your option so that your options end useless, and you keep the option premium.

Selling put options carries the danger of significant losses. Your losses limited only are to the value of the hidden shares at the strike cost. This will take place if the value of the underlying stock is up to zero.

When selling options put into ensuring you can fulfill your obligations on the occasion of workout, you are needed to supply a margin.

You are in danger of exercise at any time; the option is in-the-money. You should only offer put options over stocks that you would be comfy buying at the strike cost.

The three primary strategies for selling put options are:

- Provide an income source from the option premium use your extra capital

- Purchase shares at a discount rate to your target price.

The most popular strategy for offering put options is to produce an income from the option premium. This involves speculating on the marketplace value of the stock underlying remaining above the price strike of the option.

You can always close your option position before a workout and before expiration if you want to avoid the danger of your exercised option being.

You can use capital spare as margin when selling put options as a short-term measure to earn additional income. You can offer put options as a method to buy stocks at your target cost. You choose the options based upon the stock you wish to purchase and the strike cost at your target purchase cost. You accomplish your objective in buying the stock and maintain the option premium if your options are worked out.

There are two risks in utilizing put options to acquire stocks at your target rate. The stock price might rise, and you miss out on getting in, or the stock rate may fall significantly, and you are required to purchase the stock well above the market rate.

CHAPTER THIRTEEN

Options Trading Frames Time

Time frames are an integral part of options trading and require to be given mindful factors to consider when initiating any investment. Timespan is represented with charts such as those that will be laid out in the next chapter. There is a countless amount of time, as they can range from as brief as one hour to several months long. It depends on the investor to analyze the time frames to forecast how the market will move and hence if the financier requires to offer or purchase options.

What precisely requires to be examined? That the trendline would be, which is detailed in the time frame chart. By looking at the table, a financier will have the ability to inform if it is bearish or bullish and, using the trade signals discussed in the next chapter, when the marketplace is going to continue or reverse its pattern. There is not just one pattern that investors need to be worried with. There are three trends: primary, intermediate, and term in brief.

Every security underlying can be represented with these patterns, which are reputable depending upon the length of their time frame, Having a longer time frame.

It allows investors to track the pattern of a hidden stock more precisely. Consider example a 3-month very long time frame versus a 5-minute timespan. The 5-minute frame would reveal a tiny portion of the possession's pattern, which may be an abnormality when taking a longer timespan trend into account or perhaps might appear incorrect, depending on just how much noise is happening in regards to that specific possession. Therefore, considering that a long-term pattern is more reputable, it is the most accurate for locating the primary trend.

The main pattern ought to always be the financier's central issue. This is not since it is the just one worth focusing on. On the contrary, various trends will be used by different kinds of investors, such as a day trader versus a position trader. When it comes to the position trader, it would be smart to make the primary trend a priority since it focuses on long-lasting time frames and, after that, make smaller sized earnings using the intermediate-and short-term frames. To this in juxtaposition, a day trader would mainly use the main pattern as an umbrella for the short amount of time she or he would mostly deal with as calls and puts are quickly traded. It is, therefore, best for a starting investor to focus on the work she or he would most like to do and then find the suitable timespan for it, continually basing calculations off of the primary trend. This can be achieved by utilizing the short-term pattern in connection with the faster amount of time and the investor's preferred time frame for the intermediate-trend, all while tracking the primary trend in the long period frame.

In line with the concept of tailoring timespan and securities to a financier's options, the two timespans passed by as the investor's primary issue ought to be used to match the principal amount of time. Depending upon how the investor selects to use the time frames, the financier could gain benefits on three separate levels, enacting a lot of the strategies talked about in the previous chapter. For instance, a financier might hold a long position on a stock using the primary trend to forecast movements within the market for that particular underlying financial investment, likewise referred to as the underlying pattern. As soon as this has been identified, the investor uses whatever amount of time is most suited to his/her style of trading (brief for day trading, long for position trading, etc.) to figure out the intermediate trend pattern. The financier then generates a short-term model to implement strategies that may satisfy any variety of functions. These might include utilizing the short-term trend and time frame to develop insurance for the extended position, to enjoy benefits with calls or puts as the pattern varies, or any other of the numerous usages of short-term trends and time frames. How the time frames are made use of is entirely up to the individual financier and therefore is a versatile method to increase and create earnings utilizing the investor's natural trading strengths.

One word of caution must be kept in mind relating to the short-term trends. Frequently, since they are so little, short-term charts can end up being overcrowded with a high volume of financiers and trigger the table to appear very volatile when, in fact, it is not. Financiers should beware not to over-analyze the chart and regularly compare it with the main pattern in words of Investopedia author Joey Fundora, "Short-term charts are typically used to validate or dispel a hypothesis from the primary chart" (Fundora, Multiple Time Frames). It is those hypotheses drawn from the contrast of the first and short-term charts that lead investors to make reasonable forecasts relating to the market and implementing options trading methods from there.

Since there is timespan consisting of trends that represent all underlying properties, neophyte options traders can typically become puzzled by the inconsistent details. State, for example, the main pattern for the stock of business XYZ in a very long time frame shows the stock is bullish. Nevertheless, when the investor looks at a short-term trend on two days, the stock appears to be entirely bearish without any apparent signs of a rally. The investor must not worry and begin to offer all of his/her shares; instead, the financier should realize that the short-term pattern is merely a little of the primary trend portion. Which, if it is a pattern continuation, will keep its bullish outlook and continue to climb up the chart. To see from this example is easy to see why the company and a clear understanding of options trading before entering the service are invaluable tools.

Among the keys to growing a portfolio is to concentrate on the future patterns of the marketplace rather than the past. Many financiers who are either novices or extremely frightened of losing cash rely purely on past information given by extended period frames, rather than focusing on how the trend might be the future act. This is where signals in trading, detailed in the next chapter, end up being extremely beneficial. The factor they are being discussed here is since it is essential for financiers always to be looking towards the future. While seasoned financiers might do their best to show the truth to the contrary, the marketplace is a fickle animal, and not every relocation can be predicted and upon acted. If that were so, no one would lose ever, which would naturally result in a complete market crash. Trends do reverse and change; it depends on the investor to understand the patterns and make informed decisions as to how to act upon the direction.

CHAPTER FOURTEEN

Trading Signals and Trading Signal Providers

Trading on the stock exchange can be overwhelming. With many prospective contracts out there, it's tough for traders to understand which ones they need to sell or buy and which ones they must release by. In times of trade increase and volatility within the marketplace, traders count on trade signals to help identify their next relocation. Trade signals mainly originate from technical signs, which are "any class of metrics whose value is derived from generic rate activity in a stock or possession ... Technical indications are used most extensively by active traders in the market, as they are developed primarily for analyzing short-term cost movements" (Investopedia, Technical Indicator). These might be available in the type of various charts that develop different shapes, such as a wedge, rectangular shape, or triangle, which will suggest to the trader what movement will happen in the market for a specific underlying security. Also, charts might form bullish or bearish pennants, which further enables traders to figure out the worth of options and predict motions within the marketplace. In this chapter, various signals will be analyzed, and descriptions will be offered to demonstrate how investors may use signs to their advantage. The half of the first chapter will be devoted to kinds of signals, while the latter half will focus on trading signal service providers. If this sounds a bit like a hokey fortune-teller reading tarot cards, do not stress; similar to all things in the market, it's quite technical. The last recommendation is to look at the old main trendlines on very long time frames to get a concept of where trade signals turn up and how the market reacts to them. With practice, investors will be able to spot the chart signs easily.

Flag

This very first example of a trading signal is relatively easy to comprehend. A flag sign is a boxy fit, concise, and generally inclines in the opposite direction of the market pattern. It represents a moment briefly when the market breathes and stays relatively neutral before continuing the trend it had been going on previous to the flag. This moment of calm before continuing the pattern is called the combination period. After spotting the banner on a bullish continuation pattern, investors may decide to start purchasing calls, given that the trade rate is low and financiers expect it to increase per the trend. Identify a flag on a trendline by trying to find anywhere two parallel lines completely frame the visual market pattern.

Pennant

This chart is a short-term chart extension pattern. With a pennant pattern, asymmetrical triangle points its peak at the market pattern increase or reduction, depending on whether the trend is bullish or bearish, respectively. In basic, a pennant is formed just after a flag symbol, and subsequently, it is, in some cases, referred to as a flag pennant. Because the objective of a trading signal is to forecast when it is a great time to buy or offer, utilizing a bearish or bullish pennant pattern to predict market trends can, even more, notify which techniques to use to maintain or appreciate possessions.

Rectangular shape

The rectangular shape trade signals are incredibly similar to a flag with one exception: unlike the flag, the rectangular shape signal has a lot longer and more resistant consolidation period. This essentially suggests that during the combination period, financiers might have a hesitant mindset towards the marketplace. The trend will measure the state of mind of participants (a.k.a. willingness to sell and buy), which results in a regular horizontal pattern firmly compacted in between the sharp market trends. When looking at a trendline, investors will quickly have the ability to see where long rectangular shape boxes in the lines and will use it to make market predictions.

Triangle

There are three types of triangle patterns: rising, symmetrical, and descending. These correlate to a neutral, bullish trend and bearish, respectively. According to authors Chad Langager and Casey Murphy at Investopedia, "The basic construct of this chart pattern is the convergence of two trendlines-flat, rising or descending-with the cost of the security moving in between the two trendlines" (Langager, Murphy, Analyzing Chart Patterns). [9] Depending upon the nature of the trendline, in addition to the resistance and support

(meaning whether financiers feel the trading cost will move down or up) happening within the triangle, investors may pick to hold long or brief positions upon the breakout, which is when the trendline abandons the triangle pattern.

Wedge

Wedges fall under two classifications: falling and rising. These appearances in a bullish or bearish can then make a pattern. The tricky element of the wedge is that for a newbie, it will look like the market cost will continue to increase in the beginning glance. Once the trendline outbreaks of the wedge, it will maybe moving in direction opposite as when the wedge it was. This means that investors, generally speaking, spotting upon a wedge, know that the market is going to begin moving in the other instructions. That is the minute lots of financiers will begin starting new methods to make the most of the market change.

Head-and-Shoulder This signal is used to figure out when a trend is going to become tired and reverse itself. It portrays a precise balance within the market as sellers bring the trendline down, and purchasers press it back up once again. This signal indicative can be of an upward or downward pattern, depending upon the current market climate. Usually, the market will rally three times; after the last shoulder (or third peak), the trend will reverse its bullish or bearish position. Like other signals, financiers can use this info to purchase or offer calls and puts as essential.

Some beginning investors who are daunted by trade indications elect to enter of online signal providers whom financiers can pay to look out of any possible significant shifts in the market, which an investor can then use to his or her benefit. As the saying goes, absolutely nothing in this world comes for totally free. Trade signal companies can cost a hefty amount of cash since the best trade signal providers take risk management into account. And offer clients a selection of packages that will arrange each person's needs in terms of trade interests, investments, and beginning capital.

Investors must always be wary when signing up for services from signal companies. The Internet is cluttered with frauds, and generally, an allegedly relied on signal supplier appears as mere false months after being touted as one of the most excellent signal companies available. When a supplier provides services complimentary of charge, a clear caution indication that a financier is stepping into a fraud is.

Furthermore, fraudulent websites will need the trader to invest a specific quantity of capital, which the trader is then sure to lose. Even if the financier thinks he or she has found a protected site, in-depth research must be carried out before buying a membership to any signal provider website. The dangers are far too excellent to stroll into a contract blindly and are comparable to trading options before reading a book about it.

CHAPTER FIFTEEN

This chapter will take account of all of the information currently discussed and put it in a step-by-step guide for novice financiers in options trading. Naturally, individuals might originate from the strategy; however, they want; this is merely an example of actions to take that describes the options open to investors. Amateur yet well-informed traders will have the ability to contend in options trading in no time if this fundamental summary is followed. Additional ideas are listed at the end of the chapter to assist financiers in preventing the mistakes of options trading, therefore leading them to portfolio gratitude.

Selecting a Security can be done by investigating the financing areas of significant news corporations. A basic search will show up outcomes such as CNN's Money section, which notes the most active companies according to the S&P 500. It would be wise to look for out the guidance of a buddy or mentor if the investor is already partly immersed in the financing world. New options traders, and especially those who are new to trading in basic, should approach options trading cautiously. Rather than diving right in, investors must get their feet wet by exploring a limited variety of securities and options so that they can monitor gains and losses and prevent errors for future investments.

Pick OTC or Regulated Trading while this can be decided at a later stage, it is suggested here so that new financiers can describe the boards of a controlled exchange such as the New York Exchange stock. When choosing a call or put that is well matched to their tastes, practiced traders can pick up an OTC option later on if wanted, such as a call to cover the expense of insurance put, likewise referred to as a married put.

Select Strategies Before starting trading, financiers will require to be sure they recognize with a few basic strategies that can be implemented with a stock. Without these strategies, options will simply sit with the financier being none the wiser or well equipped to get profit. Recommended techniques are the long call, bull call spread, and bear put spread, short straddle, and long straddle. A lot of other strategies are built on the base of these 5; subsequently, mastering them will enable the investor to become more advanced in his or her approach and, therefore, trades. There is one method that needs to be settled at the beginning of the organization endeavor, and that is the exit strategy.

Financiers need to decide ahead of time what they can manage to lose, which will be determined by their net capital upon entering the trade, and if they are willing to lose it. The reason this is so essential is since if the stock price drops below the strike cost for an investor's put, they could incur unlimited debt.

If this halfway happens through the life of the option contract, the investor will require to decide if they wish to ride the stock cost out or instantly acquire a call to help offset the put.

Whatever the financier chooses to do, it is essential not to panic ought to trade not work out, and even if it is working out, the trader needs to have an exit strategy continually. In the words of the senior analyst in options Brian Overby, "You need to choose in advance your upside exit point and your disadvantage exit point, along with the timeframes for each exit" (Overby, How to Avoid the Top 10 Mistakes New Options Traders Make).

 Continuously have a strategy, stick to it, and ideally, losses will not ever be too considerable.

Analyze the Market Investors will require to study the time frame charts connected with their underlying security options. Consider all three patterns in concerns to the time frame and note how the security is moving within each. Investors must attempt to make a forecast relating to how the design will run in the future utilizing the trade signals gone over in the previous chapter. These investors will be lead to the next step.

Purchase Options and Trade Finally, the minute investors have been waiting for. Based upon conclusions drawn from studying timespan charts, financiers will require to purchase the suitable calls or puts. At the very same time, financiers must choose one or two of the strategies which they are currently familiar with that they think will work well in today market environment.

If trading via a controlled exchange, options for the methods might be picked from a list published by the transfer, the investor will not just need to choose a call versus put. However, likewise, if American vs. Europeans want to trade options, long vs. short, and plain vanilla vs. exotic. For a new options trader, Plain and American vanilla options are strongly advised as the previous is quicker available, and the recent deals fewer complications. The combination of the 2 is most likely to gain rewards for somebody brand-new to options trading. Once the suitable options have been chosen for the excellent method, investors will be able to execute their preparation for options trading success by buying or offering their possibilities. From there, it's all as much as the marketplace!

Using a strategy called"One Size Fits All," This is never, ever real. Since the marketplace is continuously changing, techniques should continuously alter. A married put going to work not at every time frame, if just for the fact that it gains such minimal revenue. When selecting methods for particular underlying properties and time frames, financiers require to be sensible.

Doubling Risk to Cover Loss Taking this method is comparable to a gambler getting in a poker game with an all-or-nothing state of mind after having just lost everything in his wallet. Methods can either fail or acquire capital, and financiers require to be sure they are not attempting to overcompensate for the loss by investing in a bad trade. If a specific strategy is not working, the investor would be best off deserting it all together as quickly as he or she is able, utilizing the financier's individualized exit technique.

Greed Though it's to be exciting on the uptrend and gaining financial benefits through options trading, it's critical for investors to realize when they require to go back. This is where having an exit technique on the uptrend comes in since; eventually, the market will reverse itself, and investors do not want to be captured losing all of their robust generated income on the downswing just because they got a little greedy.

This can be partially offset by continually analyzing the time frame charts and searching for trade signals. When doing so, financiers must not just search for new opportunities, however likewise end up being conscious of prospective fiscally damaging scenarios.

Concentrating On One Asset Once the investor has gotten his/her "sea legs" in concerns to options trading, it is essential to diversify those options.

A portfolio needs to include numerous properties, and while managing multiple options and strategies simultaneously may be daunting to newbie investors, it is imperative not to put all of the eggs in one basket. As quickly as the financier feels comfy, they must take on brand-new underlying possessions and develop their portfolio.

Neglecting Future Trends A typical mistake amongst brand-new financiers is to confuse historical patterns with future ones. Past models are only a sign of future trends in that their shapes can be used to predict a change in the model, which is what the pennant, flag, rectangular shape, triangle, wedge, and head-and-shoulders signals are used for. Puzzling the two will lead financiers to make unreliable predictions and hence lose money on faulty techniques. Instead, investors should practice finding future chances by examining old timespan charts, which will hone their skills and acquire them future incomes.

Options trading is a fantastic method to construct a portfolio and earn capital. With time, brand-new investors will find out and make mistakes to correct them. Ideally, with this step-by-step guide and ideas for errors to avoid, investors will feel great entering the world of options trading and taking on the market.

Conclusion.

Trading options do not need to be complicated; in truth, it can be as complicated or straightforward as the specific trader wants it to be. Similar to any other investment tool, options trading ought to be in every investor's tool kit. Having the ability to use such versatile methods and options opens up doors to higher financial chance, which is the principle that the entire investment industry rests on. So, either the trader is brand new to the world of investment or a skilled expert looking to broaden their horizons. Options trading must consistently be considered as a premier financial investment tool that can be used to shape an investor's future into one filled with chance, convenience, and monetary stability.